SANJEEV KAPOOR

Simply Stylish

ENTERTAINING AT HOME

In association with Alyona Kapoor

www.popularprakashan.com

Published by:

POPULAR PRAKASHAN PVT. LTD.

301, Mahalaxmi Chambers

22, Bhulabhai Desai Road

Mumbai 400 026

for **KHANA KHAZANA PUBLICATIONS PVT. LTD**.

(4008)

ISBN – 978-81-7991-260-7

Cover Design: Mahendra Ghanekar

Book Design: Pratibha Gurnani Creative

Photography: Bharat Bhirangi & Alim Bolar

Food Stylist: Anupa Das

Printed in India by

Thomson Press (India) Ltd.

Author's Note

There is nothing I enjoy more than cooking up a meal for family and friends. Not only because I am a chef, but food cooked for those whose company I enjoy always seems to take on an extra-special flavour that can only come from the sheer pleasure of presenting a gift from the heart and receiving appreciation for the effort.

For many, entertaining at home can be a bit of a chore. Today's fast pace of life, juggling professional and family commitments, often prompts one to take the easy way out: order food from the nearest take-away, or treat one's guests to the food at the latest 'in' restaurant. Both perfectly good options, but as we all know, a bit of a compromise on the real thing: entertaining at home with all the personal care that goes into a home-cooked meal, served in the comfort of one's own home.

Style, for me, has a lot to do with the personal connection Alyona and I have both with the food we serve and our guests. The simplest dish can be made special and elegant not only by the presentation, but also by the warmth with which it is offered. Colour, texture, variety and taste, all play a part in one's selection of the best menu to put together for any occasion, but nothing can replace the personal touch.

In Simply Stylish Entertaining at Home, I have described some of the favourite dishes we offer our guests. Try out the many dishes and select the ones best suited to the occasion. I have included a large variety to suit practically any event – intimate dinners, large boisterous family gatherings, chilled-out evenings with friends, or sophisticated evenings designed to impress. All you have to do is follow the recipes and remember each one serves four persons. Above all, keep it simple and do it in style!

Happy Cooking!

contents

green lady

Ingredients

8 tablespoons *khus* syrup

A pinch of salt

2 tablespoons lemon juice

4 glasses lemonade

4 lemon slices

Crushed ice

Method

❶ Mix together the *khus* syrup, salt and lemon juice.

❷ Add the crushed ice and lemonade and stir well.

❸ Garnish with a slice of lemon.

❹ Serve chilled.

virgin pina colada

Ingredients

1¾ cups unsweetened pineapple juice

8 tablespoons thick coconut milk

8 tablespoons shredded tender coconut flesh

2 cups vanilla ice cream

8 tablespoons chopped pineapple chunks

16-20 tinned cherries, drained

Crushed ice as required

Method

❶ Process together the pineapple juice, coconut milk, coconut flesh, vanilla ice cream and ice in a blender till smooth.

❷ Pour into individual Collins glasses.

❸ Serve immediately, decorated with the pineapple chunks and cherries.

tropical fruit and nut smoothie

Ingredients

1 apple
2 ripe mangoes
2 bananas
85 grams golden raisins
12-16 pistachios, chopped
Crushed ice, as required

Method

❶ Peel and core the apple and cut into slices.
Peel and chop the mangoes. Peel and slice
the bananas. Place the fruits in a freezer till frozen.
❷ Process the frozen apple, mango and banana
slices with the golden raisins and crushed ice in
a blender. Pour into individual tall glasses.
❸ Serve chilled, garnished with the chopped
pistachios.

imli ka amlana

Ingredients

4 tablespoons tamarind pulp
1½ teaspoons black salt
⅓ teaspoon black pepper powder
⅓ teaspoon green cardamom powder
1 teaspoon roasted cumin powder
3 teaspoons roasted carom seed powder
6 tablespoons sugar
Salt to taste
8-10 fresh mint leaves, roughly chopped

Method

❶ Add five cups of water to the tamarind pulp and mix well.
❷ Grind together the black salt, pepper powder, cardamom powder, cumin powder, carom seed powder, sugar and salt to a very fine powder.
❸ Add the mixture to the tamarind water and mix well.
❹ Decorate with the fresh mint leaves and serve chilled.

When it comes to cooling homemade drinks, *Imli Ka Amlana* is a summer favourite.

ginger lemonade

Ingredients

2 inches ginger, grated
3 tablespoons lemon juice
1 cup sugar
4 lemon slices
Ice cubes as required

Method

❶ Combine the ginger and sugar with two cups of water in a pan. Bring the mixture to a boil, stirring continuously until the sugar dissolves. Simmer for three minutes.
❷ Strain the syrup through a piece of muslin and set aside to cool.
❸ Combine the syrup with two and a half cups of water. Add the lemon juice and stir well.
❹ Pour into individual tall glasses. Add the ice cubes and decorate each glass with a lemon slice. Serve immediately.

kokum and anar slush

Ingredients

1⅓ cups *kokum* syrup
4 tablespoons pomegranate kernels
2 teaspoons roasted cumin powder
2 teaspoons black salt
8 tablespoons sugar
4 cups crushed ice

Method

❶ Process the *kokum* syrup, roasted cumin powder, black salt, sugar and crushed ice in a blender until slushy.
❷ Pour into individual glasses and serve, decorated with a sprinkling of the pomegranate kernels.

The cocktail/mocktail circuit makes excellent use of grenadine which is thickened and sweetened pomegranate juice. Here pomegranate kernels add visual appeal and texture to the cooling and appetite-whetting *kokum* slush.

coconut refresher

Ingredients

2 whole tender coconuts
2 apples, peeled and cored
8 tablespoons sugar syrup
2 tablespoons lemon juice
4 apple fans for garnishing

Method

❶ Chill the whole tender coconuts thoroughly. Slice off the tops, drain the water and scoop out the flesh.
❷ Chop the apples roughly. Process the coconut water with the coconut flesh, apples, sugar syrup and lemon juice in a blender until smooth.
❸ Pour into individual glasses. Decorate with the apple fans and serve chilled.

red pumpkin soup

Ingredients

1 kilogram red pumpkin, diced

1 tablespoon butter

3 bay leaves

15-20 black peppercorns

3 large onions, sliced

4 cups Vegetable Stock (page 126)

Salt to taste

1 teaspoon white pepper powder

1 tablespoon lemon juice

¼ cup cream (optional)

Method

❶ Heat the butter in a pressure cooker; add the bay leaves and peppercorns. Add the onions and sauté for two minutes.

❷ Add the diced pumpkin and sauté for half a minute. Add four cups of water and cook under pressure until the pressure is released once (one whistle).

❸ Strain and reserve the stock. Purée the vegetables.

❹ Add the reserved stock and one cup of water to the purée.

❺ Add the salt and white pepper powder and bring to a boil. Stir in the lemon juice.

❻ Serve hot, garnished with cream.

Chef's Tip: This soup can be served in the shells of scooped out small red pumpkins, no bigger than the size of a coconut.

palak aur tofu shorba

Ingredients

500 grams fresh spinach leaves

100 grams tofu, diced

1 teaspoon oil

4-5 black peppercorns

½ teaspoon cumin seeds

1 medium onion, chopped

½ inch ginger, chopped

2-3 garlic cloves, chopped

Salt to taste

1 tablespoon lemon juice

Method

❶ Blanch the spinach leaves in plenty of boiling water. Drain and refresh in cold water.

❷ Heat the oil in a pan. Add the peppercorns and cumin seeds and fry until they start to change colour. Add the onion and sauté for two minutes.

❸ Add the ginger and garlic to the pan and sauté until golden.

❹ Purée the blanched spinach leaves with half a cup of water in a blender. Add the spinach purée to the pan with enough water to give a good consistency. Add the salt and bring the mixture to a boil.

❺ Add the lemon juice. Finally, add the tofu to the soup and serve immediately.

I confess that this is a take-off on the popular spinach and *paneer* combination. For those who haven't eaten tofu before, it takes some getting used to. Start off with this soup and then gradually add more tofu recipes to your repertoire.

mushroom cappuccino

Ingredients

15 large fresh button mushrooms, thickly sliced

1 tablespoon butter

1 bay leaf

1 small onion, chopped

4-6 garlic cloves, chopped

4 cups Vegetable Stock (page 126)

Salt to taste

¼ teaspoon white pepper powder

¼ cup cream

2½ cups milk, chilled

1 teaspoon cinnamon powder

Method

❶ Melt the butter in a heavy-bottomed pan. Add the bay leaf, onion and garlic and sauté for two to three minutes or till the onion becomes translucent.

❷ Add the mushrooms and sauté for a minute. Add one cup of vegetable stock and cook for five more minutes. Remove from heat and cool. Discard the bay leaf.

❸ Make a purée of the cooked mushrooms. Add the remaining vegetable stock to it.

❹ Return to heat and bring it to a boil. Add the salt and white pepper powder and allow the soup to simmer for two to three minutes.

❺ Add the cream and half a cup of milk and remove from heat. Pour the soup into individual cups. Set aside.

❻ Pour the remaining chilled milk into a chilled bowl.

❼ Beat the milk with a fork till it produces a froth. Collect the froth with a ladle and place it on the hot mushroom soup giving it a cappuccino effect.

❽ Sprinkle cinnamon powder and serve immediately.

Chef's Tip: Whole milk will produce better froth.

I had once surprised my guests by serving them this soup in large mugs while they were eating their starters. They actually thought coffee was being served and were reluctant to drink it till I explained!

minestrone toscano with pesto crôute

Ingredients

2 tablespoons macaroni

3 cups Vegetable Stock (page 126)

1 medium potato, cut into small pieces

1 medium carrot, cut into small pieces

3-4 French beans, cut into small pieces

Salt to taste

½ teaspoon white pepper powder

¼ small cabbage, shredded

1 medium zucchini, cut into small pieces

2 tablespoons tomato concassé (see below)

½ cup tomato purée

1½ tablespoons oil

6-8 garlic cloves, chopped

1 medium onion, chopped

¼ teaspoon crushed dried oregano

10-12 fresh basil leaves, hand torn

¼ cup grated Parmesan cheese

Method

❶ Bring the vegetable stock to a boil in a deep pan. Add the macaroni and potato and cook on medium heat for a minute.

❷ Add the carrot and French beans and continue to cook. Add the salt and white pepper powder and mix.

❸ Add the cabbage, zucchini, tomato concassé and tomato purée.

❹ Heat the oil in a non-stick pan. Add the garlic and onion and sauté till translucent. Add the oregano and continue to sauté. Add to the soup cooking in the pan and mix.

❺ Add the basil leaves and continue to simmer till the vegetables are cooked.

❻ Sprinkle Parmesan cheese and serve piping hot with pesto crôute (see below).

Notes:

• To make the tomato concassé, blanch the tomatoes; peel them, remove the seeds and chop roughly.

• To make the pesto crôute, toast the bread slices and spread with pesto.

• You can also serve the soup with garlic bread or breadsticks.

Busy cooks are grateful for chunky soups! Serve in deep bowls as a one-bowl satisfying meal.

clear lemon coriander soup

Ingredients

2¾ teaspoons lemon juice

½ teaspoon grated lemon rind

3 tablespoons chopped fresh coriander

1 medium carrot, cut into ½-inch pieces

2-3 ears of babycorn, cut into
½-inch pieces

¼ small head broccoli, separated into florets

¼ small Chinese cabbage, cut into ½-inch pieces

2-3 fresh button mushrooms, sliced

1 tablespoon oil

1 spring onion, chopped

2 garlic cloves, chopped

4 cups Vegetable Stock (page 126)

Salt to taste

4-5 black peppercorns, freshly crushed

¼ teaspoon MSG (optional)

Method

❶ Blanch the carrot, babycorn and broccoli in boiling water for one minute. Drain, refresh in cold water and set aside.

❷ Heat the oil in a wok; add the spring onion and garlic and sauté on medium heat for half a minute. Add the Chinese cabbage and mushrooms and stir-fry on high heat for two minutes. Stir in the vegetable stock and bring to a boil.

❸ Add the blanched vegetables and cook on high heat for one minute. Stir in the salt, peppercorns, lemon rind and MSG, and continue cooking for another minute.

❹ Add the lemon juice and fresh coriander. Stir to mix and serve hot.

Lemon and Coriander Soup is fast becoming popular in many restaurants replacing the one-time favourite thick sweetcorn soup.

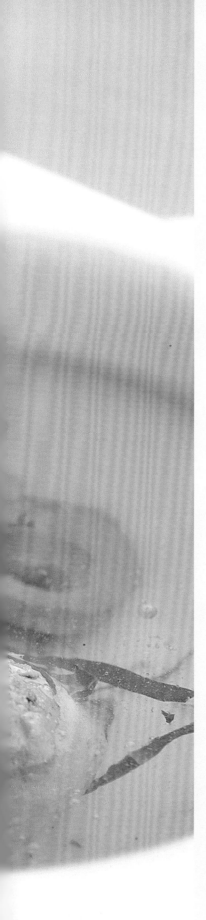

prawn ball soup

Ingredients

250 grams prawns, shelled, deveined and minced

3-4 tinned bamboo shoot slices

Salt to taste

Black pepper powder to taste

1 tablespoon cornflour

1 egg white, beaten

1 tablespoon oil

1 inch ginger, chopped

5-6 medium fresh button mushrooms, sliced

5-6 black peppercorns, crushed

4 cups Chicken Stock (page 126)

10-12 fresh spinach leaves

2-3 stalks spring onion greens, chopped

Method

❶ Boil the bamboo shoots in two cups of water for three to four minutes. Drain and cut into strips. Set aside.

❷ Add the salt and pepper powder to the prawns and mix. Add the cornflour and egg white. Mix well. Take a teaspoonful of the mixture and shape into a small ball. Repeat with the remaining mixture.

❸ Heat the oil in a wok and sauté the ginger for half a minute. Add the bamboo shoot slices, mushrooms, crushed peppercorns, salt and chicken stock and bring to a boil.

❹ Add the prawn balls and cook for two to three minutes. Add the spinach leaves and simmer for a minute.

❺ Serve hot, garnished with spring onion greens.

Poached prawn dumplings with spring onion greens and bamboo shoots make a superlative soup! Try this out when the theme is Oriental food.

chicken coconut rasam

Ingredients

500 grams chicken bones

100 grams boneless chicken, skinned and cut into 1-inch cubes

½ cup grated coconut

3 tablespoons tamarind pulp

2 medium tomatoes, roughly chopped

Salt to taste

2 tablespoons *rasam* powder

8 black peppercorns, crushed

1 teaspoon red chilli powder

½ teaspoon turmeric powder

15 curry leaves

2 tablespoons chopped fresh coriander

1 tablespoon oil

1 teaspoon mustard seeds

2-3 dried red chillies, broken into two

Method

❶ Grind the coconut with one cup of warm water. Extract the coconut milk and set aside. Reserve the coconut residue.

❷ Boil the chicken bones in about six to seven cups of water for fifteen minutes.

❸ Skim off the scum from the surface, add the tamarind pulp, tomatoes, chicken cubes, salt, *rasam* powder, crushed peppercorns, chilli powder, turmeric powder, and ten curry leaves and continue cooking.

❹ Simmer till the liquid reduces by half and gives out a pleasant aroma.

❺ Add the drained coconut residue to the *rasam*. Sprinkle the fresh coriander and simmer for about three to four minutes.

❻ Remove from heat and strain the *rasam*. Separate the chicken pieces from the residue and cut into half-inch cubes and reserve for garnishing.

❼ Reheat the strained *rasam*, add the coconut milk and simmer for a couple of minutes. Remove from heat and add the chicken pieces.

❽ Heat the oil and temper it with the mustard seeds, dried red chillies and remaining curry leaves. Add to the prepared soup and cover immediately to trap the flavours.

❾ Serve piping hot. Add some lemon juice to make it really tangy.

Rasam is best had during the monsoon and winter, as the spices that go into making the *rasam* powder fill your body with warmth. Make this powder in bulk and store in an airtight container and use it not only in *rasam* but to flavour *dal* as well.

balinese vegetable soup

Ingredients

225 grams French beans, cut into ½-inch pieces

Salt to taste

2 cups thin Coconut Milk (page 126)

1 garlic clove

2 fresh red chillies, chopped

4 almonds

½ tablespoon coriander powder

1½ tablespoons oil

1 medium onion, sliced

2 bay leaves

1⅓ cups bean sprouts

2 tablespoons lemon juice

Method

❶ Cook the French beans in six cups of boiling water with salt for three to four minutes. Drain and reserve the cooking liquid.

❷ Grind together the garlic, red chillies, almonds and coriander powder to a paste.

❸ Heat the oil in a non-stick wok; add the onion and sauté till translucent. Drain and set aside.

❹ To the same oil, add the ground paste and sauté without browning for about two minutes.

Add the reserved cooking liquid and the coconut milk. Bring to a boil and add the bay leaves. Cook uncovered for fifteen to twenty minutes.

❺ Just before serving add the beans, sautéed onion, bean sprouts and lemon juice. Adjust the salt and serve immediately.

For those who prefer a soup and salad meal, this is a good start. French beans and bean sprouts add a chewy texture that is very satisfying.

red onion, tomato and pasta salad

Ingredients

1 large red onion, thinly sliced

4 medium tomatoes, quartered and seeded

3 cups short pasta of different shapes, cooked *al dente*

1 medium yellow capsicum, roasted

2 small zucchinis, sliced

Salt to taste

A few sprigs of fresh basil, to garnish

Dressing

2 tablespoons oil

1½ tablespoons red wine vinegar

1 teaspoon Dijon mustard

½ teaspoon caster sugar

Salt to taste

12-15 black peppercorns, crushed

½ cup roughly torn fresh basil leaves

Method

❶ Cool the capsicum, peel and slice into strips.

❷ Blanch the zucchini and refresh in cold water.

❸ Mix together all the ingredients for the dressing.

❹ Drain the pasta well and transfer to a large serving bowl. Add the dressing and toss well.

❺ Add the capsicum, zucchini, onion and tomatoes; toss well to mix.

❻ Cover the bowl and leave to stand at room temperature for about thirty minutes to allow the flavours to develop.

❼ Serve, garnished with sprigs of basil.

salade niçoise

Ingredients

1 head of iceberg lettuce

4 medium potatoes, boiled and diced

15 French beans, blanched and
cut into 2-inch pieces

4 medium tomatoes, quartered

4 hard-boiled eggs, quartered
and yolks separated

¼ cup French Dressing (see below)

10 black olives, stoned

Method

❶ Tear the lettuce into bite-size pieces
and place in iced water.

❷ Place the potatoes, French beans,
tomatoes and egg whites in a large bowl.
Toss once to mix.

❸ Pour the French dressing over and using two
forks, carefully toss the vegetables until they are
thoroughly coated.

❹ Arrange the chilled lettuce leaves decoratively
on a large, shallow serving platter.

❺ Spoon the salad onto the lettuce leaves and
garnish with black olives.

❻ Serve immediately.

French Dressing: Mix together ¼ cup oil, ¾
tablespoons vinegar, ½ teaspoon mustard
powder, ¼ teaspoon freshly crushed black
peppercorns and salt to taste in
a jar; close tightly and shake well to mix.

coriander prawns
with mango salad

Ingredients

¾ cup small prawns, peeled, deveined and headless

½ cup Green Chutney (page 126)

1 small unripe mango, peeled and
cut into thin strips

2 medium tomatoes

1 teaspoon mustard paste

Salt to taste

4-5 tablespoons sugar

4-5 black peppercorns, crushed

1 teaspoon lemon juice

4-5 iceberg lettuce leaves, placed in iced water

Method

❶ Halve the tomatoes, remove the seeds and cut into strips.

❷ Marinate the prawns in the green chutney for about fifteen minutes.

❸ Heat a *tawa* and cook the prawns till tender.

❹ Mix together the unripe mango strips, tomato strips, mustard paste, salt, sugar, crushed peppercorns, lemon juice and one tablespoon of water.

❺ Add the grilled prawns and toss to mix.

❻ Serve on a bed of iceberg lettuce.

This combination of prawns and mango is unique.

cottage cheese and pineapple salad

Ingredients

300 grams cottage cheese,
cut into ½-inch cubes
½ small fresh pineapple, cut into ½-inch cubes
1 large unpeeled cucumber, cut into 1-inch pieces
1 medium green capsicum, cut into 1-inch pieces
½ small head of iceberg lettuce
6-8 black olives, stoned and sliced
1 teaspoon garlic paste
1 tablespoon lemon juice

1 teaspoon red chilli powder
½ teaspoon mixed dried herbs
Salt to taste
1½ tablespoons oil

Dressing
1½ tablespoons salad oil
4 tablespoons vinegar
1 teaspoon sugar
1 teaspoon mustard powder
5-6 black peppercorns, crushed
½ teaspoon white pepper powder

Method

❶ Combine the garlic paste, lemon juice, chilli powder, dried herbs and salt. Rub the mixture into the cottage cheese pieces and set aside to marinate, preferably in a refrigerator, for fifteen to twenty minutes.
❷ Mix together all the ingredients for the dressing in a bowl.
❸ Thread the cottage cheese cubes onto skewers. Heat the oil on a griddle and place the skewers on it. Cook, turning the skewers a few times, to brown the cottage cheese evenly on all sides. Remove the cottage cheese pieces from the skewers and transfer onto a plate and set aside to cool.
❹ Combine the grilled cottage cheese, pineapple, cucumber, capsicum, roughly torn iceberg lettuce and olives in a large serving bowl. Drizzle the dressing over and toss to mix well. Serve immediately.

tabbouleh

Ingredients

4 tablespoons cracked wheat

4 spring onions

1 cup fresh parsley, roughly chopped

1 tablespoon fresh mint, chopped

1 tomato

1 tablespoon lemon juice

Salt to taste

¼ teaspoon black pepper powder

2 teaspoons olive oil

Method

❶ Soak the cracked wheat for about fifteen minutes; drain.

❷ Chop the spring onion bulbs and greens separately.

❸ Place the soaked cracked wheat in a bowl. Add the chopped spring onion bulbs and mix, crushing the onions slightly with your fingers.

❹ Add the chopped parsley and mix well.

❺ Add the chopped spring onion greens and fresh mint.

❻ Quarter the tomato, scoop out the seeds and cut into small cubes. Stir into the salad.

❼ To make the dressing, mix together the lemon juice, salt and pepper powder. Pour over the salad and mix well. Add the olive oil and toss to mix.

❽ Chill and serve.

kachumber

Ingredients

1 medium tomato, cut into ½-inch pieces

1 medium cucumber, cut into ½-inch pieces

1 medium green capsicum, cut into ½-inch pieces

½ medium white radish, cut into ½-inch pieces

1 medium carrot, cut into ½-inch pieces

1 medium onion, chopped

2 green chillies, chopped

2 tablespoons chopped fresh coriander

1 tablespoon lemon juice

Salt to taste

Method

❶ Mix together the tomato, cucumber, capsicum, white radish and carrot in a bowl. Add the onion, green chillies, fresh coriander, lemon juice and salt.

❷ Toss well.

❸ Arrange in a salad bowl and serve cold.

bread salad with diced chicken

Ingredients

3-inch piece of French loaf, cut into small cubes
2 boneless chicken breasts, skinned, boiled and cut into small cubes
2 tablespoons oil
1 tablespoon vinegar
2-3 garlic cloves
½ cup fresh basil leaves + a few for garnishing
Salt to taste
2 medium tomatoes, seeded and cut into small pieces
1 large cucumber, seeded and cut into small pieces
4 lettuce leaves

Method

❶ Preheat an oven to 180°C/350°F/Gas Mark 4.
❷ Spread the bread cubes in a shallow baking dish and bake in the preheated oven for ten minutes, or until crisp and golden. Remove from the oven and set aside.
❸ Combine the oil, vinegar, garlic, basil leaves and salt in a food processor and blend at high speed for a few seconds to make a coarse paste. Transfer to a large bowl.
❹ Add the bread cubes, chicken, tomatoes and cucumber, and toss well. Let the salad stand for five minutes to allow the bread to soften slightly.
❺ Line a serving dish with the lettuce leaves and transfer the salad into it. Garnish with basil leaves and serve immediately.

potli kabab

Ingredients

4 boneless chicken breasts, skinned

250 grams chicken mince

2 tablespoons ginger-garlic paste

2 tablespoons chopped fresh coriander

5-8 fresh mint leaves, chopped

2 green chillies, chopped

Salt to taste

½ cup drained (hung) yogurt

2 tablespoons gram flour

2 tablespoons cream

1 teaspoon green chilli paste

½ teaspoon *garam masala* powder

1 tablespoon melted butter, for basting

Method

❶ Slit the chicken breasts without cutting through. Open them out. Flatten slightly with a steak hammer or with the back of a knife.

❷ Marinate the chicken mince with one tablespoon ginger-garlic paste, fresh coriander, fresh mint, chopped green chillies and salt for about fifteen minutes.

❸ Divide the mince mixture into four equal portions and shape them into balls. Place a ball on a flattened chicken breast. Close the breast around the ball.

❹ Place the yogurt in a bowl. Add the gram flour, remaining ginger-garlic paste, salt, cream, green chilli paste and *garam masala* powder and mix well.

❺ Marinate the stuffed chicken balls in the mixture for two hours, preferably in the refrigerator.

❻ Preheat an oven to 200°C/400°F/Gas Mark 6.

❼ Thread the balls horizontally, an inch apart, onto skewers.

❽ Cook in the preheated oven for twenty minutes basting with melted butter a few times in between. You can also roast them in a moderately hot *tandoor* for eight to ten minutes. Baste with melted butter and cook for another three to four minutes.

❾ Transfer to a plate. Serve hot with salad and chutney.

Chef's Tip: If the chicken mince is not very fine, process it it in a blender a couple of times.

36

sabudana thalipeeth

Ingredients

1 cup sago, soaked
2 medium potatoes, boiled, peeled and mashed
2-3 green chillies, chopped
¼ teaspoon red chilli powder
½ cup crushed roasted peanuts
2 tablespoons chopped fresh coriander
1 tablespoon cumin seeds
Salt to taste
1 teaspoon oil
4-5 teaspoons ghee

Method

❶ Mix together the sago, mashed potatoes, green chillies, chilli powder, roasted peanuts, fresh coriander, cumin seeds and salt.
❷ Divide the mixture into four portions and form each portion into a ball.

❸ Grease a thick plastic or polythene sheet with a little oil and place the *sabudana* ball on it. Flatten the ball with moistened or greased fingers into a thick round.
❹ Heat a non-stick *tawa* and add a teaspoon of ghee. Gently transfer the *thalipeeth* onto the *tawa* and peel the plastic off. Cook, spreading both sides with a teaspoon of ghee till evenly light golden brown.
❺ Serve hot with chutney.

Chef's Tip: Cut open a clean plastic milk pouch and roll out the *thalipeeth* on it.

paneer-stuffed papad rolls

Ingredients

8 (eight-inch) *papad*
150 grams cottage cheese,
cut into ½-inch cubes
1-2 green chillies, chopped
½ teaspoon red chilli powder
½ teaspoon cumin powder
1 teaspoon *chaat masala*
2 tablespoons chopped fresh coriander
½ inch ginger, chopped
Salt to taste

Method

❶ Mix together the cottage cheese, green chillies,
chilli powder, cumin powder, *chaat masala*, fresh
coriander, ginger and salt.
❷ Cut each *papad* into half. Roast each half directly
over a flame or on a hot *tawa* and shape into a cone
immediately.
❸ Arrange the cones in a deep bowl and stuff them
with the cottage cheese mixture.
❹ Serve immediately.

Food presentation means a lot to me. These cones are
easy to make but hold a lot of promise. You can stuff
them with different types of fillings and add variety to
your starters' list.

tiranga paneer tikka

Ingredients

450 grams cottage cheese

4 tablespoons Green Chutney
(page 126)

2½ tablespoons grated *khoya/mawa*

5-6 saffron threads

Salt to taste

½ tablespoon red chilli powder

1 cup drained (hung) yogurt

2 tablespoons gram flour

1 tablespoon ginger-garlic paste

4 tablespoons chopped fresh coriander

3-4 green chillies, chopped

1 tablespoon white pepper powder

1½ tablespoons lemon juice

Melted butter for basting

Method

❶ Grate one hundred grams of the cottage cheese and cut the remaining into one and a half inch cubes. Slice each cube into three layers without cutting through.

❷ In a bowl, mix the *khoya*, saffron and salt. In another bowl, mix the grated cottage cheese, chilli powder and salt.

❸ On each cottage cheese cube, spread the green chutney on the first layer, *khoya* mixture on the second layer and the grated cottage cheese mixture in the third layer.

❹ Mix together the hung yogurt, gram flour, ginger-garlic paste, fresh coriander, green chillies, white pepper powder and lemon juice in a deep bowl. Add the stuffed cottage cheese cubes and mix gently so that all the cubes are evenly covered with the marinade. Set aside to marinate for about an hour.

❺ Thread the cubes onto skewers keeping sufficient distance between each and roast in a *tandoor* or over a charcoal grill at a moderate temperature for five to six minutes. You can also cook them on a hot *tawa*. Baste them with melted butter once in between.

❻ Serve hot with onion rings and lemon wedges.

Chunky and tri-coloured, these look really special with a touch of India's colours.

sandwich dhokla

Ingredients

1 cup rice

¼ cup split, skinless black gram

¼ cup yogurt

Salt to taste

2 teaspoons ginger paste

1½ teaspoons green chilli paste

½ teaspoon soda bicarbonate

1 tablespoon lemon juice

½ cup thick Green Chutney

(page 126)

2 tablespoons chopped fresh coriander

Method

❶ Dry-roast the rice and gram on medium heat for four to five minutes. Cool and grind into a moderately coarse powder.

❷ Place the powder in a bowl, and add the yogurt and one and a half cups of warm water. Mix thoroughly to make a batter of pouring consistency.

❸ Add the salt and leave it to ferment for eight to ten hours.

❹ Add the ginger and green chilli pastes to the fermented batter and mix well.

❺ Bring some water to a boil as in a *dhokla* steamer.

❻ Pour half the batter into a separate bowl. In a small bowl, mix one-fourth teaspoon of soda bicarbonate and half a tablespoon of lemon juice. Add to the batter and whisk well. Repeat this procedure for the remaining batter just before putting it into the steamer.

❼ Pour the batter into a *thali* and place it in the steamer. Steam for eight to ten minutes.

❽ Test for doneness with a knife. If the knife comes out clean, it is cooked.

❾ Remove from the steamer and spread green chutney over the *dhokla* while hot.

❿ Pour the remaining batter over the chutney and steam again for ten minutes.

⓫ Remove from the steamer, cool slightly, and garnish with fresh coriander.

⓬ Cut into desired shapes and serve hot.

kadai prawns with roasted pepper jam

Ingredients

400 grams large prawns, shelled and deveined

4 dried red chillies, broken into large bits

1 teaspoon coriander seeds

2 tablespoons lemon juice

Salt to taste

1½ tablespoons oil

1 teaspoon carom seeds

1 medium onion, chopped

1 teaspoon ginger-garlic paste

2 green chillies, chopped

½ teaspoon roasted and crushed

dried fenugreek leaves

¾ cup roasted pepper jam

2 tablespoons chopped fresh coriander

½ teaspoon *garam masala* powder

Roasted Pepper Jam

4 medium red capsicums, quartered

2 medium tomatoes, seeded and quartered

Salt to taste

1 teaspoon oil

3-4 garlic cloves, chopped

3 tablespoons cider vinegar

2 tablespoons brown sugar

2 teaspoons red chilli flakes

Method

❶ Preheat an oven to 180˚C/350˚F/Gas Mark 4.

❷ To make the roasted pepper jam, arrange the red capsicums and tomatoes on a baking tray. Sprinkle salt over them. Bake in the preheated oven for twenty to twenty-five minutes and set aside to cool. When cold, peel the skin of the red capsicums and tomatoes and purée in a blender.

❸ Heat the oil in a non-stick pan; add the garlic and sauté for thirty seconds. Add the capsicum-tomato purée and cook for two minutes. Stir in the vinegar and bring to a boil. Simmer and add the brown sugar, chilli flakes and salt. Cook till the quantity reduces to half. Remove from heat and set aside.

❹ Dry-roast the red chillies and coriander seeds. Cool and grind coarsely.

❺ Marinate the prawns in the ground *masala*, lemon juice and salt for fifteen minutes.

❻ Heat the oil in a pan and add the carom seeds. When they splutter, add the onion and sauté till golden brown. Add the ginger-garlic paste and green chillies and sauté for thirty seconds.

❼ Add the marinated prawns and stir-fry for a few minutes. Add one-fourth cup of water and cook till the prawns are tender. Add the *kasoori methi* and mix well.

❽ Add the roasted pepper jam and mix till all the prawns are coated well with the jam.

❾ Garnish with the fresh coriander and *garam masala* powder and serve hot.

I find this an ideal party dish. The pepper jam can be prepared much in advance. No need to rush on the day of the party. The rest of the recipe is so simple that it is ready in the blink of an eye.

steamed cabbage rolls

Ingredients

8 cabbage leaves, trimmed

200 grams boneless, skinless chicken

6 medium (200 grams) prawns, shelled and deveined

1 teaspoon cornflour

½ teaspoon red chilli powder

Salt to taste

1 egg, lightly beaten

1 tablespoon oil

1 leek, sliced

1 garlic clove, sliced

2 fresh red chillies, sliced

Method

❶ Blanch the cabbage leaves in hot water for two minutes. Drain and pat dry with absorbent paper.

❷ Mince the chicken and prawns in a food processor. Transfer to a bowl and add the cornflour, chilli powder, salt and egg. Mix well.

❸ Place two tablespoons of this mixture towards one end of each cabbage leaf. Fold the sides around the filling and roll up.

❹ Bring to boil sufficient water in a steamer. Arrange the cabbage rolls, seam-side down in a single layer on a slotted plate. Place it in the steamer and steam for ten minutes.

❺ Heat the oil in a wok and sauté the leek and garlic for two minutes. Set aside.

❻ Transfer the steamed rolls onto individual serving plates and garnish with fresh red chilli slices. Serve with the sautéed leek and garlic.

dahi idli

Ingredients

1 cup parboiled rice

½ cup skinless, split black gram

Salt to taste

2 cups yogurt, whisked

6 tablespoons honey

2 tablespoons Green Chutney (page 126)

2 tablespoons Date and Tamarind Chutney (page 126)

¼ teaspoon red chilli powder

½ teaspoon roasted cumin powder

2 tablespoons chopped fresh coriander

Method

❶ Wash the rice and soak it in three cups of water for at least two to three hours.

❷ Wash and soak the split black gram in two cups of water for a similar length of time.

❸ Drain and grind the rice to a slightly coarse texture. Use water as required to make a batter of dropping consistency. Drain and grind the skinless split black gram, sprinkling water as required to make a smooth and spongy batter.

❹ Mix both the batters together. Sprinkle salt and using your hand mix thoroughly in a whipping motion. Pour the batter into a large container, close tightly with a lid and rest in a warm place overnight.

❺ Heat sufficient water in a steamer.

❻ Place a wet muslin on an *idli* stand. Pour a spoonful of the fermented batter into each mould. Place the *idli* stand in the steamer. Cook for eight to ten minutes or till the *idli* are done.

❼ Meanwhile, mix the yogurt and honey thoroughly.

❽ Place the *idli* in a serving bowl and drizzle the sweetened yogurt and chutneys. Sprinkle the chilli powder and cumin powder.

❾ Garnish with the fresh coriander and serve.

The combination of rice and *dal* that go into the making of the *idli* – the ubiquitous South Indian snack – is nutritious too.

paneer tikka kathi rolls

Ingredients

Paneer tikka filling

1 cup cottage cheese,
cut into ½-inch cubes
2 medium tomatoes, seeded and chopped
2 teaspoons oil
2 medium green capsicums, chopped

Marinade

¼ cup yogurt, whisked
1 teaspoon red chilli powder
¼ teaspoon turmeric powder
½ teaspoon ginger paste
¼ teaspoon garlic paste
1 tablespoon gram flour
½ teaspoon *chaat masala*
½ teaspoon dried fenugreek leaves
½ teaspoon *garam masala* powder
Salt to taste

Chapati

1 cup wholewheat flour
¼ cup milk
Salt to taste

Method

❶ Mix together all the ingredients for the marinade
in a deep bowl. Add the cottage cheese and
tomatoes and toss lightly. Marinate for ten minutes.
❷ Heat the oil in a non-stick pan. Add the capsicums
and sauté for two minutes.
❸ Add the marinated cottage cheese mixture and
sauté over high heat for four to five minutes, stirring
occasionally. Cook till the moisture dries and set aside.

❹ For the *chapati,* combine all the ingredients and
knead into a soft dough. Divide the dough into
eight equal portions. Roll out each portion into
a thin *chapati.*
❺ Heat a *tawa* and cook each *chapati* lightly on
both sides. Set aside.
❻ Divide the *paneer tikka* filling into eight equal
portions.
❼ Place one portion of the filling in the centre of
each *chapati* and roll up tightly.
❽ Before serving, cook the rolls on a hot *tawa*
till warm. Cut into two-inch long pieces and
serve hot.

Spicy *mazedaar* soft *paneer* in even softer *chapati*...
you will love this recipe. It is a good idea for packed
lunches too.

jhaal muri

Ingredients

2 cups puffed rice

1 medium onion, chopped

¼ cup sprouted whole black Bengal gram, boiled

1 small cucumber, cut into 1-inch cubes

1 small tomato, seeded and cut into 1-inch cubes

2 green chilles, chopped

2 tablespoons roasted peanuts, skinned

2 tablespoons chopped fresh coriander

2 tablespoons mustard oil (taken from a pickle)

2 tablespoons *Jhaal Muri Masala* (see below)

¼ fresh coconut, sliced, to garnish

Method

❶ In a large bowl, combine the puffed rice, onion, sprouted *chana*, cucumber, tomato, green chillies, peanuts and fresh coriander and toss to mix well.

❷ Add the mustard oil and *jhaal muri masala* and toss again to mix well. Serve immediately, garnished with sliced coconut.

Notes:

• For the *jhaal muri masala*, mix together 1 teaspoon rock salt, 1 tablespoon roasted cumin power, ½ tablespoon chilli powder, 1 teaspoon *chaat masala* and ½ teaspoon white pepper powder.

• If you do not have a pickle containing mustard oil then heat 2 tablespoons of mustard oil to smoking point. Take it off the heat, add ½ teaspoon mustard seeds, ¼ teaspoon fenugreek seeds, ¼ teaspoon fennel seeds, ½ teaspoon red chilli powder and a pinch of asafoetida. Leave to stand for an hour, strain and use.

Jhaal is spicy in Bengali and *Muri* is murmura. *Jhaal Muri* is a popular street food of Kolkata. If your chilli tolerance is high go for more pickle oil and *masala* because there are always *rosogullas* to follow!

khaas seekh

Ingredients

1 cup grated cottage cheese

600 grams minced chicken

1½ teaspoons green cardamom powder

1 tablespoon *garam masala* powder

1 tablespoon chopped fresh mint

1 egg

Salt to taste

1 teaspoon white pepper powder

1 tablespoon oil

1 teaspoon *chaat masala*

Chopped chutney

2 tablespoons chopped fresh coriander

2 tablespoons chopped fresh mint

2 spring onions with greens, chopped

2 green chillies, seeded and chopped

½ inch ginger, minced

3 garlic cloves, minced

Salt to taste

1 tablespoon lemon juice

Method

❶ Soak a few satay sticks in water for a while. Preheat an oven to 220°C/425°F/Gas Mark 7.

❷ Place the *paneer* in a bowl. Add half the cardamom powder, half the *garam masala* powder, and the fresh mint. Mash with your hands and mix well. Take a portion of the mixture and press it around the satay stick in a thin layer. Press the ends firmly.

❸ Place the chicken *keema* in another bowl. Break the egg into it. Add the salt, remaining cardamom powder, white pepper powder and remaining *garam masala* powder and mix well.

❹ Take a portion of the mixture and spread it over the *paneer* mixture. Similarly prepare the other *seekh*. You can chill the *seekh* in the refrigerator for some time before cooking.

❺ Meanwhile, mix all the ingredients for the chopped chutney and set aside.

❻ Bake the *seekh* in the preheated oven for ten to fifteen minutes or till tender and golden on the surface, basting with the oil in between. Alternatively, grill on a non-stick *tawa* drizzling the oil all around as they cook.

❼ Serve hot, sprinkled with the *chaat masala* accompanied by the chopped chutney.

Khaas Seekh is *khaas*, meaning special. I love this for the simple reason that it is simple to prepare.

grilled corn and capsicum toasties

Ingredients

8 slices brown bread

1 cup sweetcorn kernels, boiled

1 medium green capsicum, chopped

¾ cup grated cheese

2-3 green chillies, chopped

2 tablespoons chopped fresh coriander

1 medium onion, chopped

7-8 black peppercorns, crushed

Salt to taste

Method

❶ Preheat an oven to 180°C/350°F/Gas Mark 4.

❷ In a bowl, mix together the sweetcorn, capsicum, cheese, green chillies, fresh coriander, onion, crushed peppercorns and salt. Divide the mixture into eight equal portions.

❸ Toast the slices of bread on one side on a *tawa*.

❹ Spread the corn and cheese mixture on the other side.

❺ Place on a baking tray and bake till the topping turns golden brown.

❻ Cut each slice diagonally in half and serve hot with tomato ketchup.

tandoori
subz shaslik

Ingredients

200 grams pineapple, cut into 1½-inch cubes

2 medium green capsicums, cut into
1½-inch pieces

2 medium onions, cut into 1½-inch pieces

2 medium tomatoes, seeded and cut into
1½-inch pieces

Salt to taste

2 teaspoons red chilli powder

1½ teaspoons dried fenugreek powder

2 teaspoons *garam masala* powder

1 teaspoon *chaat masala*

2 tablespoons vinegar

1 tablespoon oil

Method

❶ In a bowl, mix together the salt, chilli powder, dried fenugreek powder, *garam masala* powder, *chaat masala*, vinegar, oil, pineapple and all the vegetables thoroughly. Set aside to marinate for one hour.

❷ Thread the pineapple, green capsicums, onions and tomatoes one after the other onto toothpicks. Pour the remaining marinade on top.

❸ Heat a non-stick *tawa*, place the toothpicks on it and cook on medium heat, turning the toothpicks a few times so that the vegetables get evenly cooked on all sides. Cook till lightly coloured.

❹ Serve hot with salad and chutney.

A delightful starter for vegetarians, especially for those who like capsicums and pineapples.

reshmi murgh tikka

Ingredients

450 grams boneless chicken legs,
cut into 1½-inch pieces
1 tablespoon oil
1 medium onion, chopped
4 garlic cloves, chopped
½ cup gram flour

First marinade

1 tablespoon ginger-garlic paste
Salt to taste
¼ teaspoon white pepper powder
½ tablespoon white vinegar

Second marinade

¼ cup cashew nut paste
½ cup melon seed paste
¼ cup cream
1 tablespoon ginger-garlic paste
Salt to taste
¼ teaspoon white pepper powder
1 tablespoon melted butter, for basting

Method

❶ Heat the oil in a non-stick pan; add the onion and garlic and sauté for a while. Add the gram flour and sauté slightly taking care that the colour of the gram flour does not change. Set aside to cool.
❷ For the first marinade, mix together the ginger-garlic paste, salt, white pepper powder and white vinegar and rub the mixture over the chicken. Marinade for one hour in a refrigerator.
❸ For the second marinade, place the cashew nut paste and melon seed paste in a bowl. Add the roasted gram flour mixture, cream, ginger-garlic paste, salt and white pepper powder and mix.
❹ Rub the mixture over the marinated chicken and marinate again for three hours in the refrigerator.
❺ Preheat an oven to 200°C/400°F/Gas Mark 6.
❻ Thread the marinated chicken onto skewers and cook in the preheated oven for ten minutes basting with melted butter once in between. Flip the sides, baste with melted butter and cook the other side for ten minutes. Alternatively, roast the pieces in a *tandoor* or over a charcoal grill for six minutes, or until half done. Baste with the melted butter and roast for another three to four minutes.
❼ Serve hot with salad and chutney.

The silken texture of the *kabab* is what gave it the name! The double marination makes the chicken more tender and creamy.

prawn varuval

Ingredients

12-16 medium prawns, shelled and deveined
1 inch ginger
6-8 garlic cloves
1 teaspoon roasted cumin powder
1 tablespoon tamarind pulp
2 teaspoons red chilli powder
½ teaspoon turmeric powder
2 tablespoons rice flour
Salt to taste
2 tablespoons oil
1 tablespoon lemon juice

Method

❶ Grind the ginger and garlic to a fine paste.
❷ Mix together the ginger-garlic paste, roasted cumin powder, tamarind pulp, chilli powder, turmeric powder, rice flour, salt and one tablespoon oil.
❸ Marinate the prawns in the mixture for at least two hours, preferably in a refrigerator.
❹ Heat the remaining oil in a non-stick pan; add the marinated prawns and cook for a minute on high heat. Turn over the prawns and cook for another minute. Reduce heat and cook for two to three minutes, turning the prawns occasionally for uniform cooking.
❺ Drain on absorbent paper. Sprinkle lemon juice and serve hot.

Simple to make, great to taste, they are ideal starters with cocktails. They can also be served with rice and *rasam*.

tandoori chaat

Ingredients

1 medium green capsicum, cut into
1½-inch cubes
1 medium red capsicum, cut into
1½-inch cubes
1 medium onion, cut into 1½-inch cubes
¼ small fresh pineapple, cut into 1-inch cubes
200 grams cottage cheese,
cut into 1½-inch cubes

Marinade
1½ tablespoons melted butter
1 tablespoon *chaat masala*
1 teaspoon red chilli powder
Black salt to taste
1 tablespoon lemon juice

Garnish
2 tablespoons chopped fresh mint
¼ cup pomegranate kernels
½ tablespoon *chaat masala*

Method

❶ Combine all the ingredients for the marinade in a large bowl.

❷ Add the green and red capsicums, onion and pineapple to the marinade and mix so that all the pieces are coated evenly. Allow to marinate for ten minutes.

❸ Preheat an oven to 180°C/350°F/Gas Mark 4.

❹ Add the cottage cheese cubes to the marinated ingredients and toss gently to mix.

❺ Thread the marinated ingredients one after the other onto skewers and grill them in the preheated oven for ten minutes. Remove and set aside to cool.

❻ Remove from the skewers into a large bowl, add the fresh mint, pomegranate kernels and *chaat masala* and toss well to mix.

❼ Serve immediately.

The sweetness of fresh vegetables and fruit in a *chaat* form... the colourful capsicums add to the flavour and appearance.

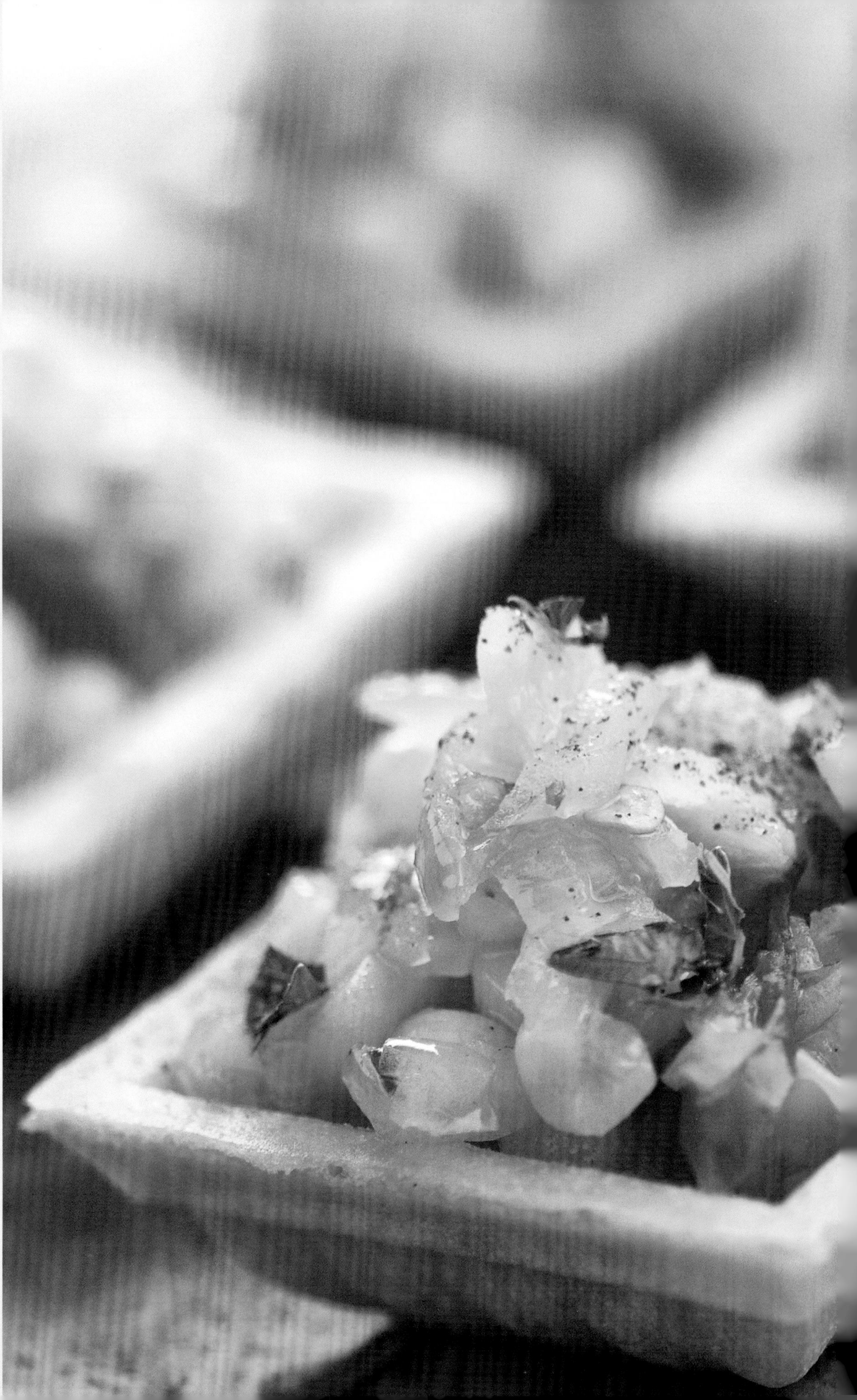

american sev puri

Ingredients

1 cup American sweetcorn, boiled
¼ cup *sev*
24 canapés
1 tablespoon oil
1 medium onion, chopped
2 fresh red chillies, chopped
¼ cup sweet chilli sauce
½ teaspoon *chaat masala*
1 tablespoon chopped fresh mint
2 tablespoons chopped fresh coriander
1 tablespoon lemon juice
2 tablespoons chopped fresh parsley

Method

❶ Heat the oil in a pan. Add the onion and sauté. Add
the sweetcorn and sauté. Add the red chillies and sweet
chilli sauce and toss. Add the *chaat masala*, fresh mint and
coriander. Mix and cook till dry. Set aside to cool.
❷ Grill the canapés using the grill mode in a microwave oven
till crisp. Set aside to cool.
❸ Add the lemon juice to the corn mixture. Place the corn
mixture in the canapés. Sprinkle *sev*. Garnish with parsley and
serve immediately.

keema kulcha

Ingredients

1½ cups minced mutton
1 cup refined flour
1 cup wholewheat flour
Salt to taste
¼ teaspoon soda bicarbonate
2 tablespoons milk
2 tablespoons yogurt
3-4 garlic cloves, crushed
1 inch ginger, chopped
2 green chillies, chopped
1 medium onion, chopped
4 tablespoons chopped fresh coriander

Method

❶ Sift the refined flour and wholewheat flour along with the salt and soda bicarbonate into a bowl. Add the milk and yogurt and mix. Add sufficient water and knead into a soft dough. Cover with a damp cloth and set aside for fifteen minutes. Divide into eight equal portions.

❷ Add the garlic, ginger, green chillies, onion, fresh coriander and salt to the minced mutton and mix well. Divide into eight equal portions.

❸ Roll out each portion of dough into a *puri*, place one portion of minced mutton mixture in the centre, gather in the edges and roll into a ball. Roll the ball into a thin round disc or *kulcha*.

❹ Heat a pressure cooker. Apply a little water on one side of the *kulcha* and stick onto the inner wall of the cooker. Similarly stick on two more *kulcha*. Invert the cooker over the flame and cook on medium heat for two to three minutes.

❺ Remove the *kulcha* with a pair of tongs and serve hot.

Serve *kulcha* with mint chutney and sit back for the compliments!

corn and coriander rice

Ingredients

¾ cup tinned corn kernels

6 tablespoons chopped fresh coriander

1 cup Basmati rice, soaked

1 tablespoon oil

2-3 garlic cloves, chopped

2 green chillies, seeded and chopped

Salt to taste

1 tablespoon lemon juice

Method

❶ Cook the rice in three cups of water until just done. Drain thoroughly and spread on a large plate to cool.

❷ Heat the oil in a non-stick *kadai*; add the garlic and sauté for a minute.

❸ Add the chillies, rice, corn kernels, fresh coriander, salt and lemon juice and sauté on high heat for two to three minutes, tossing continuously.

❹ Transfer to a serving bowl and serve hot.

Short of time? A dish that can be cooked in a jiffy and titillates the taste buds too.

bhare baghare tamatar

Ingredients

8 medium firm red tomatoes

1 tablespoon unsalted butter

5-6 fresh button mushrooms, chopped

½ cup grated cottage cheese

1½ tablespoons grated processed cheese

½ medium red capsicum, chopped

2 teaspoons chopped fresh coriander

2 green chillies, chopped

12 cashew nuts, halved

Salt to taste

½ cup raw shelled peanuts

2½ tablespoons oil

2 medium onions, sliced

¼ teaspoon mustard seeds

¼ teaspoon cumin seeds

½ teaspoon caraway seeds

8 curry leaves

1½ tablespoons ginger paste

1 tablespoon garlic paste

¼ cup tamarind pulp

1 teaspoon red chilli powder

½ teaspoon turmeric powder

2 teaspoons coriander powder

½ teaspoon roasted cumin powder

Method

❶ Blanch the tomatoes in boiling salted water for half a minute. Drain and peel. Slice off the top of each tomato and scoop out the seeds to make cups.

❷ Heat the butter in a pan and sauté the mushrooms until all the moisture evaporates. Remove and cool.

❸ Mix together the mushrooms, cottage cheese, processed cheese, capsicum, fresh coriander, green chillies, cashew nuts and salt.

❹ Spoon the mixture into the tomato cups and set aside.

❺ Roast the peanuts, cool and grind with a little water into a fine paste.

❻ Heat two tablespoons of oil in a non-stick pan and sauté the onions till golden brown. Drain on absorbent paper.

❼ Add the remaining oil to the pan and heat. Add the mustard seeds, cumin seeds and caraway seeds and sauté till they begin to splutter.

❽ Add the curry leaves and sauté for half a minute. Add the ginger paste and garlic paste and sauté until lightly browned.

❾ Stir in the tamarind pulp and sauté for three to four minutes on medium heat.

❿ Add the fried onions, chilli powder, turmeric powder, coriander powder and cumin powder and continue to sauté till the oil rises to the surface.

⓫ Add the peanut paste and sauté until the mixture thickens.

⓬ Add three cups of water and salt, bring to a boil and lower heat.

⓭ Carefully add the stuffed tomatoes to the simmering gravy and cook for four to five minutes. Do not overcook the tomatoes; they should be firm and hold their shape.

⓮ Serve hot.

When it comes to making something as simple as a ripe tomato into an exotic dish, this recipe will win hands down! With the rich cheesy stuffing and the peanut-flavoured gravy, it is worth all the effort it takes.

hare chane aur paneer ki sabzi

Ingredients

200 grams shelled fresh green *chana*

150 grams cottage cheese, cut into small pieces

1 inch ginger

8 garlic cloves

1 tablespoon oil

½ teaspoon cumin seeds

4 medium onions, grated

3 large tomatoes, grated

Salt to taste

1 teaspoon red chilli powder

¾ teaspoon roasted cumin powder

1 teaspoon coriander powder

2 tablespoons chopped fresh coriander

½ teaspoon *garam masala* powder

Method

❶ Grind the ginger and garlic together to a paste.

❷ Heat the oil in a non-stick *kadai* and add the cumin seeds. When they begin to change colour, add the onions and sauté till light brown.

❸ Add two tablespoons of water to the ginger-garlic paste and mix. Once the onion turns brown add the mixture and stir. Add the tomatoes and sauté for ten to fifteen minutes, or till the oil rises to the surface.

❹ Add the *hare chane* and one and a half cups of water and bring to a boil. Add the salt, chilli powder and roasted cumin powder and stir. Cover and cook on medium heat for fifteen to twenty minutes, or till tender.

❺ Add the coriander powder and mix. Add the fresh coriander, cottage cheese and *garam masala* powder and simmer for two minutes.

❻ Serve hot.

Fresh green *chana* is seasonal and is excellent on its own or mixed with other foods. Here *paneer* and *hara chana* make a great combination.

karela
andhra-style

Ingredients

4-5 medium (250 grams) bitter gourds
Salt to taste
1 inch ginger
5 garlic cloves
4 dried red chillies
1 tablespoon coriander seeds
1 teaspoon cumin seeds
1 teaspoon sesame seeds
1½ teaspoons oil
2 medium onions, chopped
¼ cup tomato purée
2 tablespoons grated jaggery
2 tablespoons tamarind pulp

Method

❶ Wash, scrape the outer skin, and cut the bitter gourds in half lengthways. Remove the seeds and slice thinly. Apply the salt and set aside for ten to fifteen minutes. Wash with plenty of water, drain and squeeze out the excess water.

❷ Grind the ginger and garlic together to a fine paste.

❸ Roast the dried red chillies, coriander seeds, cumin seeds and sesame seeds on a medium hot *tawa* till light brown, stirring continuously. Cool the spices and grind to a fine powder.

❹ Heat the oil in a non-stick pan; add the bitter gourd and sauté for four to five minutes or till slightly browned. Add the onions and sauté for three to four minutes.

❺ Add the ginger-garlic paste and stir-fry for one to two minutes. Add the tomato purée and cook for a few minutes longer.

❻ Add the ground spice powder, jaggery, tamarind pulp and salt. Stir well and add one cup of water and bring to a boil. Reduce the heat to medium, cover and cook for five minutes.

❼ Serve hot.

chole dhania masala

Ingredients

¾ cup chickpeas

¼ cup split Bengal gram

1½ teaspoons coriander seeds

50 grams fresh coriander

½ inch cinnamon

1½ teaspoons cumin seeds

1 black cardamom

4-5 cloves

Salt to taste

2 green chillies

2 tablespoons ghee

1 medium onion, sliced

1 teaspoon garlic paste

1 teaspoon ginger paste

½ tablespoon dried mango powder

½ teaspoon *garam masala* powder

Black salt to taste

¼ teaspoon red chilli powder

Method

❶ Soak the chickpeas and split Bengal gram separately for four to six hours. Drain, mix, add three cups of water and a little salt and pressure-cook till the pressure is released five to six times (five to six whistles).

❷ Lightly roast and powder the cinnamon, cumin seeds, coriander seeds, black cardamom and cloves. Grind together the fresh coriander and green chillies to a smooth paste.

❸ Heat one and a half tablespoons ghee in a non-stick *kadai*; add the onion and sauté for three to four minutes or till golden. Add the garlic paste and ginger paste and continue to sauté for another minute.

❹ Add the spice powder, dried mango powder, *garam masala* powder, black salt and coriander paste and sauté for two to three minutes, or till the ghee separates from the *masala*.

❺ Add the chickpeas and split Bengal gram and mix. Add half a cup of water if the mixture is too dry. Adjust salt and let the mixture come to a boil. Reduce heat and simmer for four to five minutes.

❻ Heat the remaining ghee in a small pan, take it off the heat and add the chilli powder and immediately pour over the *chana*. Cover immediately and let it stand for five minutes.

❼ Serve hot with *roti*.

diwani handi

Ingredients

3 medium potatoes, cut into ½-inch cubes

3 medium carrots, cut into ½-inch cubes

10-12 French beans, cut diagonally

10-12 broad beans, cut diagonally

4-6 small brinjals, slit

½ cup shelled green peas

1½ tablespoons oil

2 medium onions, sliced

2-3 green chillies, seeded and chopped

1 tablespoon ginger paste

1 tablespoon garlic paste

1 teaspoon red chilli powder

½ teaspoon turmeric powder

Salt to taste

2 tablespoons yogurt

½ bunch fresh fenugreek, chopped

2 tablespoons chopped fresh coriander

½ teaspoon *garam masala* powder

Method

❶ Heat the oil in a *handi*; add the onions and sauté on medium heat till light brown. Add the green chillies, ginger paste and garlic paste and sauté for a minute. Add the chilli powder, turmeric powder and salt and mix.

❷ Add the yogurt and stir-fry for two to three minutes.

❸ Add all the vegetables and simmer, covered, till the vegetables are cooked.

❹ Add the fresh fenugreek, fresh coriander and *garam masala* powder, stir and cook for three to four minutes.

❺ Serve hot with *roti.*

In olden times, this delicacy was cooked for royalty. *Handi* is a specially-designed vessel made of brass, copper or aluminium.

batata nu shaak

Ingredients

5 large potatoes

3 tablespoons oil

1 tablespoon sesame seeds, roasted

1 teaspoon red chilli powder

¼ teaspoon turmeric powder

1½ teaspoons coriander powder

1 tablespoon lemon juice

½ teaspoon sugar

Salt to taste

2 tablespoons chopped fresh coriander

Method

❶ Peel and cut the potatoes into half-inch thick round slices. Cut each slice into thin strips and soak in water. Drain thoroughly.

❷ Heat two tablespoons of oil in a non-stick pan and sauté the potatoes till golden brown. Drain on absorbent paper.

❸ Heat the remaining oil in the same pan and add the sesame seeds. When they begin to change colour, add the fried potatoes, chilli powder, turmeric powder, coriander powder, lemon juice, sugar and salt. Mix well and cook for two minutes.

❹ Garnish with the fresh coriander and serve hot.

Sweet and sour in a typical Gujarati style, it is also called *chips nu shaak*. This is an excellent accompaniment with *thepla* especially while travelling.

dahi papad
ki sabzi

Ingredients

1½ cups sour yogurt

4 Bikaneri *moong papad*

¾ tablespoon gram flour

½ teaspoon turmeric powder

¾ teaspoon red chilli powder

Salt to taste

1½ tablespoons pure ghee

1 teaspoon cumin seeds

1½ teaspoons coriander powder

½ teaspoon asafoetida

2 dried red chillies, broken into bits

¼ cup *boondi*

1 tablespoon chopped fresh coriander

½ teaspoon *garam masala* powder

Method

❶ In a large bowl, combine the yogurt, gram flour, turmeric powder, chilli powder and salt. Add two cups of water and whisk till smooth. Strain and set aside.

❷ Heat the ghee in a *kadai*; add the cumin seeds. When they change colour, add the coriander powder and sauté for one minute.

❸ Add the asafoetida and dried red chillies. Sauté for half a minute.

❹ Add the yogurt mixture and adjust the seasoning. Stir continuously till the mixture comes to a boil. Reduce heat and simmer for two minutes.

❺ Heat a *tawa* and roast the *papad* on both sides. Roughly break each one into two-inch pieces.

❻ Add the *papad* and *boondi* to the simmering yogurt mixture. Boil for two to three minutes.

❼ Garnish with the fresh coriander and *garam masala* powder. Serve hot.

This *sabzi* is convenient to make when you have run out of vegetables. In Bikaner, *papad* is commonly used as a vegetable!

khumb hara pyaaz

Ingredients

40 medium fresh button
mushrooms quartered

10-12 spring onions cut into
diagonal pieces

5 spring onion green stalks, chopped

12 garlic cloves, chopped

1 tablespoon rice flour

1 cup yogurt, whisked

3 cloves

3 green chillies, seeded and chopped

2 teaspoons coriander powder

Salt to taste

½ teaspoon red chilli powder

½ teaspoon turmeric powder

Method

❶ Heat a non-stick pan; add the garlic and roast for a minute on low heat. Add the mushrooms and continue cooking for three to four minutes on low heat. Add the rice flour and mix.

❷ Add the yogurt and cook till it thickens.

❸ Add the cloves, spring onions and green chillies, and continue to cook on low heat for two minutes.

❹ Add the coriander powder, salt, chilli and turmeric powders, and half a cup of water. Cook for two to three minutes. Add the spring onion greens and toss.

❺ Serve hot.

baingan bharta

Ingredients

1 kilogram large brinjals

1½ tablespoons oil

1 teaspoon cumin seeds

3 medium onions, chopped

1½ inches ginger, chopped

2 green chillies, chopped

2 teaspoons red chilli powder

Salt to taste

4 large tomatoes, chopped

2 tablespoons chopped fresh coriander

Method

❶ Wash and wipe the brinjals dry. Prick each one with a fork and roast on an open flame, in a *tandoor* or preheated oven, until the skin begins to blister and the brinjals begin to shrivel. Set aside to cool. (When in a hurry, cool the brinjals by dipping them in cold water). Peel off the skin and mash the flesh till smooth.

❷ Heat the oil in a non-stick *kadai*; add the cumin seeds and sauté till they change colour. Add the onions and sauté till translucent. Add the ginger and green chillies and sauté for one minute.

❸ Add the chilli powder and mashed brinjal and sauté for seven to eight minutes over medium heat, stirring continuously. Add salt to taste.

❹ Stir in the tomatoes and cook on medium heat for seven to eight minutes till the oil separates.

❺ Garnish with the fresh coriander and serve hot.

Chef's Tip: Add garlic to enhance the flavour of the *bharta*.

Baingan Bharta made with roasted brinjals is a North Indian speciality. In Gujarat they prefer to steam it. I enjoy both versions as they are different in taste, flavour, colour and texture. The best way to choose a large brinjal for *bharta* is to pick up one that is light in weight. It will have more flesh and fewer seeds.

dahiwale amrud

Ingredients

4 medium guavas, seeded and
cut into small pieces
½ cup yogurt
½ tbsp coriander powder
¼ teaspoon red chilli powder
¼ teaspoon turmeric powder
1 teaspoon dried mango powder
1 tablespoon ghee
2 green chillies, chopped
½ teaspoon cumin seeds
½ teaspoon fennel seeds
¼ teaspoon asafoetida
1 medium tomato, chopped
Salt to taste
¼ teaspoon *garam masala* powder
½ teaspoon sugar

Method

❶ Whisk the yogurt with the powdered spices.
❷ Heat the ghee in a non-stick *kadai*. Add
the green chillies, cumin seeds, fennel seeds
and asafoetida and stir.
❸ Add the whisked yogurt, tomatoes and salt
and stir for a while.
❹ Add three-fourth cup of water and bring to
a boil. Add the guava pieces and let the gravy
continue to boil.
❺ Lower the heat, cover and cook, stirring
occasionally.
❻ When the guavas are cooked, add the *garam
masala* powder and cook for another three to four
minutes.
❼ Sprinkle sugar and stir. Serve hot.

masala khumb

Ingredients

600 grams fresh button mushrooms, quartered

8 dried red chillies

3 teaspoons coriander seeds

1 tablespoon oil

1 teaspoon cumin seeds

2 medium onions, sliced

3 teaspoons garlic paste

4 large tomatoes, puréed

Salt to taste

4 green chillies, chopped

2 inches ginger, chopped

2 teaspoons *garam masala* powder

½ cup chopped fresh coriander

Method

❶ Roast and pound the dried red chillies and coriander seeds with a mortar and pestle to a coarse powder.

❷ Heat the oil in a non-stick *kadai*. Add the cumin seeds, onions and garlic paste and sauté for one minute over medium heat. Add the powdered spices and sauté for half a minute.

❸ Add the tomato purée and salt and sauté till the oil separates. Add the green chillies and ginger and continue to sauté for one minute. Add the mushrooms and salt and cook, stirring gently, for seven to eight minutes. Stir in the *garam masala* powder.

❹ Garnish with the fresh coriander and serve hot with *roti*.

stir-fried bean curd with lemon grass and chillies

Ingredients

675 grams firm bean curd (tofu),
cut into 1-inch cubes

2 one-inch lemon grass stalks,
bruised and chopped

2 fresh red chillies, seeded
and chopped

3 tablespoons oil

1 cup Vegetable Stock (page 126)

4 tablespoons hoisin sauce

2 tablespoons soy sauce

1½ tablespoons tomato purée

2 leeks (only the white part), sliced

1 large red capsicum, seeded and
cut into 1-inch squares

1 large green capsicum, seeded and
cut into 1-inch squares

12 button mushrooms, halved

½ teaspoon black pepper powder

Method

❶ Place the bean curd cubes between double layers of paper towels and press gently so that all the extra moisture is absorbed.

❷ Heat two tablespoons oil in a non-stick pan and sauté the bean curd cubes, a few at a time, on medium heat till golden all around. Drain on absorbent paper.

❸ Mix together the vegetable stock, hoisin sauce, soy sauce, tomato purée and fresh red chillies in a bowl.

❹ Heat the remaining oil in another non-stick wok. Add the leeks and lemon grass and stir-fry over medium heat for about one minute or till tender. Add the capsicums and mushrooms and stir-fry for a further one minute.

❺ Stir in the sauce mixture and fried bean curd and bring the mixture to a boil. Cook on medium heat, stirring frequently, for about two minutes or till the sauce thickens slightly.

❻ Transfer into a serving dish, sprinkle black pepper powder and serve immediately.

Spicy, soft and really delicious... be careful not to break the bean curd into smaller pieces. Bean curd might be delicate to handle but it is a known power food due to its protein richness. It is an excellent substitute for *paneer* in most dishes. The lactose-intolerant can enjoy the bean curd.

mangodi ki sabzi

Ingredients

200 grams green gram dumplings (*mangodi*)

2 tablespoons oil

½ cup yogurt

2 tablespoons gram flour

Salt to taste

1 teaspoon red chilli powder

1 tablespoon coriander powder

½ teaspoon turmeric powder

1 bay leaf

½ teaspoon cumin seeds

2-3 dried red chillies

½ tablespoon ginger paste

2 tablespoons tomato purée

½ teaspoon *garam masala* powder

1 tablespoon chopped fresh coriander

Method

❶ Heat one tablespoon oil in a *kadai* and sauté the *mangodi* until crisp and slightly browned. Drain and set aside.

❷ Beat the yogurt, add the gram flour, salt and the chilli, coriander and turmeric powders and mix well.

❸ Heat the remaining oil in a *kadai*. Add the bay leaf, cumin seeds and red chillies and sauté.

❹ Add the ginger paste, *mangodi*, tomato purée and the yogurt mixture. Add one cup of water and mix well.

❺ Add the *garam masala* powder and fresh coriander.

❻ Cook for a few minutes and serve hot.

Another one of my favourite recipes when I am out of vegetables! *Mangodi* are small dried *moong dal* dumplings which are nutritious and a handy ingredient to store.

pumpkin foogath

Ingredients

700 grams red pumpkin, cubed

1 tablespoon oil

¼ teaspoon mustard seeds

10-12 curry leaves

2 medium onions, chopped

3 green chillies, chopped

Salt to taste

1 tablespoon grated coconut

1 tablespoon lemon juice

Method

❶ Heat the oil in a non-stick *kadai* and add the mustard seeds and curry leaves. When the mustard seeds start to splutter, add the onions and green chillies. Stir on high heat for one minute.

❷ Add the pumpkin and salt. Cook, covered, and on low heat for five to seven minutes, or until the pumpkin is cooked.

❸ Add the coconut and lemon juice and mix well.

❹ Serve hot.

I love having some fast-to-cook recipes on hand, and this stir-fry is one of them. From the chopping board to the table, I can assure you that it takes less than fifteen minutes.

mooli saag

Ingredients

4 medium white radishes with leaves
Salt to taste
2 tablespoons oil
½ teaspoon mustard seeds
½ teaspoon cumin seeds
A pinch of asafoetida
½ teaspoon turmeric powder
1 teaspoon red chilli powder
1½ teaspoons sugar
1 teaspoon dried mango powder

Method

❶ Chop the radishes into small pieces. Shred the leaves. Sprinkle a little salt on the radishes and set aside for twenty minutes. Drain off the liquid.

❷ Heat the oil in a *kadai* and add the mustard seeds. As they begin to splutter, add the cumin seeds and asafoetida and sauté for half a minute.

❸ Add the turmeric and chilli powders and sauté for ten seconds.

❹ Add the radishes and leaves and sauté for a minute. Sprinkle a little water to prevent scorching. Cover and cook on medium heat for ten minutes, or till the radish is soft and done.

❺ Adjust the salt if needed. Sprinkle the sugar and dried mango powder and mix well.

❻ Serve hot with *paranthe*.

masaledar bhindi

Ingredients

40 medium (300 grams) ladies' fingers
4 tablespoons gram flour
1 teaspoon turmeric powder
2 teaspoons red chilli powder
4 teaspoons dried mango powder
4 teaspoons coriander powder
4 teaspoons roasted cumin powder
4 teaspoons *garam masala* powder
3 tablespoons oil
Salt to taste
½ teaspoon cumin seeds
4 green chillies, chopped

Method

❶ Trim the tops and tips of the ladies' fingers and make
a slit lengthways.
❷ Mix together the gram flour and the turmeric, chilli, dried
mango, coriander, cumin and *garam masala* powders.
❸ Add one tablespoon of oil and salt and mix well.
❹ Stuff the *masala* into the ladies' fingers. Heat the remaining
oil in a non-stick *kadai* on medium heat; add the cumin seeds
and green chillies and sauté for a minute.
❺ Add the ladies' fingers and sauté for five minutes. Lower
the heat, cover and cook, stirring occasionally, till they are
cooked. Uncover and sauté till the ladies' fingers are crisp.
❻ Serve hot.

salt and pepper vegetables

Ingredients

1 medium yellow capsicum, cut into ¾-inch pieces

1 medium red capsicum, seeded and cut into ¾-inch pieces

1 medium green capsicum, cut into ¾-inch pieces

1 medium zucchini, cut into ¾-inch pieces

1 large carrot, cut into ¾-inch cubes and blanched

10-12 medium florets of broccoli, blanched

2 tablespoons oil

4 spring onions, quartered

4-inch celery stalk, chopped

3-4 garlic cloves, chopped

1 inch ginger, chopped

2 green chillies, sliced

7-8 black peppercorns, crushed

Salt to taste

¼ teaspoon MSG (optional)

1 tablespoon lemon juice

Method

❶ Heat the oil in a pan. Add the spring onions, celery, garlic and ginger, and sauté for a minute. Add the green chillies, capsicums and zucchini and sauté for two minutes.

❷ Add the carrot, broccoli, crushed black peppercorns, salt and MSG and sauté for two more minutes.

❸ Add the lemon juice and mix lightly.

❹ Serve hot.

A simple stir-fry that can brighten up your table and your day!

spinach and mozzarella lasagne

Ingredients

2 medium (700 grams) bunches spinach

2 tablespoons oil

1 medium onion, finely chopped

4 garlic cloves, crushed

4 large tomatoes, blanched, seeded
and roughly chopped

Salt to taste

5-6 black peppercorns, roasted
and crushed

¼ cup grated mozzarella cheese

¼ cup grated processed cheese

Fresh lasagne

½ cup refined flour

½ cup wholewheat flour

1 tablespoon oil

1 egg

Sauce

1 tablespoon refined flour

1 tablespoon wholewheat flour

2 tablespoons butter

2 cups milk

Salt to taste

White pepper powder to taste

Garnish

2 tablespoons chopped fresh parsley

Method

❶ Blanch the spinach and refresh under running water. Drain in a colander and squeeze to remove excess water; chop coarsely. Heat the oil in a pan; add the onion and garlic and cook until the onion softens.

❷ Add the spinach and cook till the mixture dries. Add the tomatoes and cook for about two minutes.

❸ Season with the salt and crushed black peppercorns and set aside.

❹ For the lasagne, mix the refined and wholewheat flours and salt and make a well in the centre. Add the oil and mix.

❺ Add the egg and knead into a medium hard dough. Knead lightly for five to ten minutes.

❻ Cover and rest the dough for ten minutes, then divide into three parts and roll out on a floured board into twelve-inch squares.

❼ Cut each square into six-inch-wide strips and cook in four cups of boiling salted water for three minutes. Drain the strips, immerse in cold water and set aside.

❽ Preheat an oven to 200°C/400°F/Gas Mark 6.

❾ To make the white sauce, melt the butter in a non-stick pan and add the refined flour and the wholewheat flour. Cook for two to three minutes on low heat till fragrant.

❿ Add the warm milk, whisking vigorously to avoid lumps. Add the salt and white pepper powder and cook for four to five minutes till the sauce thickens. Pass through a sieve.

⓫ In a greased ovenproof dish, spread two to three tablespoons of white sauce at the base. Arrange layers of lasagne sheets and the spinach mixture alternately, ending with the pasta as the top layer.

⓬ Pour the remaining white sauce over the top layer of pasta and sprinkle the mozzarella cheese and processed cheese. Bake in the preheated oven for about twenty minutes or till golden.

⓭ Cut into squares and serve hot garnished with the parsley.

Note: It is advisable to buy ready-made lasagne sheets which are easily available. You will save on time.

The secret of serving lasagne is to cut it up into neat squares. Italians serve it with a shaker filled with grated Parmesan to add that extra bite to the topping.

thai green curry with vegetables

Ingredients

1 medium carrot, cut into diamonds

½ small cauliflower, separated
into small florets

2-3 baby brinjals

1 medium potato, cut into ½-inch cubes

5 lemon grass stalks

1 teaspoon lemon juice

Salt to taste

¾ cup fresh coconut milk

2-3 fresh basil leaves

Green curry paste

10 green chillies

3 shallots

9 garlic cloves

1 inch galangal

3 inch lemon grass stalk

¼ teaspoon grated lemon rind

A small bunch of fresh coriander roots

2 teaspoons coriander seeds

2 teaspoons cumin seeds

Salt to taste

Method

❶ To make the green curry paste, grind the green chillies, shallots, garlic, galangal, lemon grass, lemon rind, coriander roots, coriander seeds, cumin seeds and salt to a fine paste.

❷ Blanch all the vegetables individually in boiling water and refresh in cold water. Tie the lemon grass in a piece of muslin to make a bundle. Crush it slightly.

❸ Heat a non-stick pan; add the green curry paste and roast for one minute. Add the blanched vegetables and lemon juice and cook for three to four minutes stirring continuously. Add three cups of water and continue to cook. Add the lemon grass bundle and cook for three to four minutes till the curry absorbs its flavour.

❹ Remove the bundle and add salt and coconut milk. Simmer for a minute.

❺ Add the basil leaves and take off the heat.

❻ Serve hot.

Interestingly, when Thai food first came to Indian restaurants, it was galangal that made it so customer-friendly as it is a cousin of ginger, a spice that Indians are familiar with. If galangal is not available you can use ginger.

ratatouille

Ingredients

2 medium long brinjals

2 medium zucchini

Salt to taste

1 tablespoon oil

2 medium onions, sliced into rings

4 tablespoons tomato purée

4 garlic cloves, chopped

2 medium green capsicums,
cut into thin strips

3 medium tomatoes, blanched, peeled,
seeded and chopped

¼ teaspoon coriander powder

A pinch of cinnamon powder

A few fresh basil leaves, shredded

White pepper powder to taste

Method

❶ Halve the brinjals and zucchini lengthways. Cut them again into thick slices.

❷ Place the brinjals in a colander and sprinkle with salt. Top with a heavy plate and leave to degorge for one hour.

❸ Heat the oil in a non-stick pan; add the onions and sauté over low heat until translucent. Stir in the tomato purée and cook over medium heat for three to four minutes, stirring occasionally.

❹ Rinse the salted brinjals and drain well. Add the drained brinjals and zucchini to the pan.

❺ Add the garlic and capsicums and simmer for about five minutes.

❻ Add the tomatoes, coriander powder, cinnamon powder, basil, salt and white pepper powder. Stir once or twice and cook over medium heat for about ten minutes, stirring frequently.

❼ Adjust the seasoning and serve hot.

A traditional French recipe, the vegetables are cooked in such a manner that the final dish is smooth, flavourful and luscious.

penne with creamy pesto and cherry tomatoes

Ingredients

200 grams penne, boiled

2 tablespoons cream

20 cherry tomatoes

1 tablespoon oil

2 garlic cloves, sliced

Salt to taste

5-6 black peppercorns, crushed

Pesto sauce

¾ cup fresh basil

3 tablespoons pine nuts

4 garlic cloves

2½ tablespoons oil

¼ cup crumbled Parmesan cheese

Method

❶ For the pesto sauce, grind together the fresh basil, garlic, pine nuts, oil and Parmesan cheese till smooth.

❷ Heat the oil in a non-stick pan. Add the garlic and sauté till golden. Add the cherry tomatoes, penne, salt and peppercorns and toss.

❸ Add the pesto sauce and toss. Add the cream and toss. Cook for a minute.

❹ Serve hot.

Pasta is to parties what salt is to pepper: always together! This exotic pasta is one of the toppers in my list. Just ensure that the pine nuts are fresh.

shanghai stewed noodles

Ingredients

200 grams noodles
1 tablespoon oil
6-8 garlic cloves, crushed
1 medium onion, sliced
1 spring onion, sliced
½ medium carrot, halved and sliced
4 medium fresh button mushrooms, sliced
¼ small cabbage, cut into 1-inch pieces
½ medium green capsicum, cut into
1-inch pieces
5 cups Vegetable Stock (page 126)
1½ tablespoons cornflour
¼ teaspoon MSG (optional)
½ teaspoon white pepper powder
Salt to taste
1 stalk spring onion greens, sliced
2 teaspoons Chilli Oil (page 126)

Method

❶ Heat the oil in a wok; add the garlic, onion and spring onion and stir-fry briefly. Add the carrot, mushrooms, cabbage and capsicum and continue to stir-fry for a minute.

❷ Add the vegetable stock, bring to a boil and add the noodles. Cook on high heat for two minutes. Lower the heat and simmer for four to five minutes or until the noodles are almost cooked.

❸ Mix the cornflour in half a cup of water.

❹ Stir the MSG, white pepper powder, salt to taste and the cornflour mixed in water into the noodles. Cook on medium heat for a couple of minutes or until the sauce thickens, stirring frequently.

❺ Add the spring onion greens, drizzle the chilli oil and serve hot.

Soft noodles with a saucy coating... a perfect one-dish dinner to have with that mushy serial on TV!

leeli tuvar ni kadhi

Ingredients

½ cup fresh green pigeon peas, boiled and drained

4 tablespoons gram flour

2 cups yogurt

2 tablespoons pure ghee

1 teaspoon carom seeds

4 dried red button chillies

1 inch ginger, chopped

2 teaspoons garlic paste

3 green chillies, chopped

8-10 curry leaves

A pinch of asafoetida

2 medium brinjals, diced

Salt to taste

2 teaspoons sugar

1 tablespoon chopped fresh coriander

Method

❶ Whisk the gram flour and yogurt together. Add four cups of water and whisk till smooth.

❷ Heat the ghee in a deep pan. Add the carom seeds, button chillies, ginger, garlic paste, green chillies and curry leaves and sauté for two minutes. Add the asafoetida and brinjals and sauté for two minutes.

❸ Add the boiled fresh pigeon peas and sauté for a minute. Add the yogurt mixture. Bring to a boil. Add the salt and sugar, and simmer, stirring gently, for ten to fifteen minutes or till thickened to the desired consistency.

❹ Garnish with the fresh coriander and serve hot.

Fresh, tender beans of pigeon peas are available only in the winter months. Enterprising Gujaratis store them in the freezer for use all year round.

dal lucknowi

Ingredients

1 cup split pigeon peas, soaked

2 green chillies, chopped

½ teaspoon turmeric powder

Salt to taste

1 tablespoon oil

1 teaspoon cumin seeds

4 dried red chillies, broken

5 garlic cloves, chopped

A pinch of asafoetida

1 cup milk

2 tablespoons chopped fresh coriander

Method

❶ Pressure-cook the pigeon peas and green chillies with two cups of water in a pressure cooker till the pressure is released twice (two whistles). Remove the lid when the pressure has reduced completely. Add the turmeric powder and salt and simmer on low heat.

❷ Heat the oil in a non-stick pan. Add the cumin seeds, red chillies, garlic and asafoetida and sauté till fragrant. Pour the sizzling spices into the simmering *dal* and mix well. Add one cup of water and the milk and continue to simmer for two to three minutes.

❸ Adjust the salt, garnish with the fresh coriander and serve hot.

This *dal* has a smoother and fuller texture as there is milk in it... an ingredient which will surprise many.

baingan ki kadhi

Ingredients

10-12 baby brinjals, stemmed and halved

1½ cups yogurt

1 cup gram flour

Salt to taste

½ teaspoon turmeric powder

1 teaspoon red chilli powder

1½ tablespoons ginger-garlic paste

2 medium bunches fresh fenugreek, chopped

2 medium onions, chopped

2½ tablespoons oil

¼ teaspoon fennel seeds

¼ teaspoon mustard seeds

1 teaspoon cumin seeds

¼ teaspoon fenugreek seeds

¼ teaspoon onion seeds

4 dried red chillies, broken into large bits

5-6 curry leaves

1 tablespoon chopped fresh coriander

Method

❶ In a bowl, mix together the yogurt, two tablespoons gram flour, salt, turmeric powder, chilli powder, half the ginger-garlic paste and two cups of water. Set aside.

❷ In another bowl, mix together the fresh fenugreek, remaining ginger-garlic paste, onions, remaining gram flour and salt. Mix well and form a firm dough.

❸ Heat sufficient water in a steamer. Shape the dough into small balls or *muthia* and steam for fifteen minutes or till done.

❹ Heat two tablespoons of oil in a non-stick pan. Add the brinjal pieces and sauté for three to four minutes or till cooked. Drain and set aside.

❺ Add the remaining oil to the pan. Add the fennel, mustard, cumin, fenugreek and onion seeds. When the seeds start spluttering, add the dried red chillies and curry leaves.

❻ Add the yogurt mixture and stir. Cook, till the *kadhi* thickens, stirring continuously.

❼ Add the *methi muthia* and sautéed brinjals and bring the *kadhi* to a boil again.

❽ Garnish with the fresh coriander and serve hot.

The addition of *methi muthia* is a real delight and makes this recipe fit for a party... keep a huge platter of fluffy Basmati rice alongside. The *panch phoron* (mixture of five kinds of seeds) gives the dish a unique taste.

tur dal amti

Ingredients

1 cup split pigeon peas, soaked

1 tablespoon oil

¼ teaspoon cumin seeds

1 small onion, chopped

2 green chillies

A pinch of asafoetida

Salt to taste

1 teaspoon grated jaggery

2 teaspoons tamarind pulp

½ teaspoon red chilli powder

½ teaspoon *goda masala*

1 tablespoon chopped fresh coriander

1 tablespoon grated fresh coconut

Method

❶ Pressure-cook the pigeon peas with two cups of water in a pressure cooker till the pressure is released three to four times (three to four whistles). Remove the lid when the pressure has reduced completely. Mash the *dal* with the back of a ladle.

❷ Heat the oil in a deep pan. Add the cumin seeds and sauté. When they begin to change colour add the onion, green chillies and asafoetida and sauté till lightly browned.

❸ Add the cooked *dal* and two cups of water. Mix well and bring to a boil.

❹ Lower the heat, add the salt, jaggery, tamarind pulp, chilli powder and *goda masala* and simmer for four or five minutes.

❺ Garnish with the fresh coriander and coconut and serve hot.

Amti is a sour *dal*. The *goda masala* - a Maharashtrian spice blend - is the life and soul of this flavourful dish.

lobia rassedar

Ingredients

1½ cups black-eyed beans, soaked

1½ tablespoon oil

1 teaspoon cumin seeds

½ teaspoon fenugreek seeds

2 dried red chillies

1 inch ginger

6 garlic cloves

1 inch cinnamon

2 medium onions, chopped

1 medium tomato, chopped

½ teaspoon turmeric powder

2 teaspoons red chilli powder

Salt to taste

2 tablespoons chopped fresh coriander

Method

❶ Drain and boil the beans in three cups of water until three-fourth cooked. Set aside with the cooking liquid.

❷ Heat two teaspoons of oil in a non-stick pan; add the cumin seeds, fenugreek seeds and chillies. Sauté for two minutes on low heat, stirring continuously, till fragrant. Cool and grind the spices with the ginger, garlic and a little water, to a smooth paste.

❸ Heat the remaining oil in a non-stick *kadai*. Add the cinnamon and when it begins to sizzle, add the onions and sauté on medium heat until lightly browned.

❹ Add the tomato, ground paste, turmeric powder, chilli powder and salt. Cover and cook for five to seven minutes.

❺ Add the beans along with the cooking liquid. Cover and cook till the beans are tender and gravy almost dry.

❻ Serve hot, garnished with the fresh coriander.

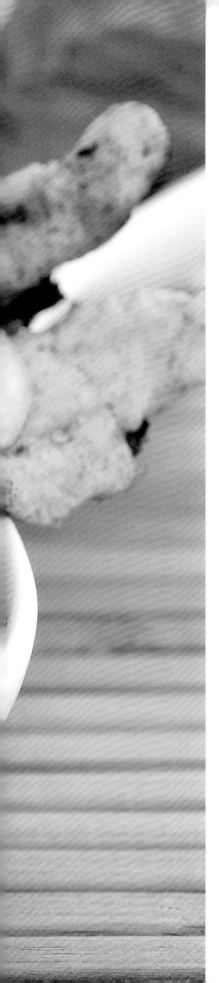

stir-fried chicken with chillies and basil

Ingredients

600 grams boneless chicken, skin removed
and cut into thin strips
6 fresh red chillies
40 fresh Thai basil leaves
2½ tablespoons cornflour
1 egg
Salt to taste
¼ teaspoon white pepper powder
2½ tablespoons oil
6 garlic cloves, sliced
3 tablespoons fish sauce
3 teaspoons dark soy sauce
1½ teaspoons sugar

Method

❶ Slice four red chillies, remove the seeds and chop. Slice the remaining two and set aside.

❷ Add the cornflour, egg, salt and white pepper powder to the chicken and mix well.

❸ Heat the oil in a non-stick wok and sauté thirty fresh Thai basil leaves. Drain on absorbent paper and set aside.

❹ In the same oil, stir-fry the marinated chicken on medium heat until crisp. Drain on absorbent paper and set aside.

❺ To the same oil, add the garlic and chopped red chillies and stir-fry for half a minute or until golden.

❻ Add the chicken, fish sauce, dark soy sauce and sugar and stir-fry for three to four minutes or until cooked.

❼ Add the remaining Thai basil leaves and mix.

❽ Serve hot, garnished with sliced red chillies and fried Thai basil leaves.

chicken laksa

Ingredients

500 grams boneless chicken, skin removed
and cut into thin strips

1 inch ginger

3-4 garlic cloves

4 shallots

1 two-inch lemon grass stalk

1½ tablespoons oil

3 cups Chicken Stock (page 126)

2 fresh red chillies, seeded and sliced

1 teaspoon curry powder

100 grams snow peas

Salt to taste

Black pepper powder to taste

1 tablespoon lemon juice

2 tablespoons Coconut Milk (page 126)

To serve

1 cup boiled noodles

2-3 spring onions, finely sliced

1 medium unpeeled cucumber, sliced

1 tablespoon chopped fresh coriander

1 tablespoon chopped fresh mint

2 lemons, halved

Method

❶ Grind the ginger, garlic, shallots and lemon grass to a paste.

❷ Heat one tablespoon of oil in a large non-stick frying pan or wok and cook the chicken over high heat until golden. Drain on absorbent paper and set aside.

❸ In the same pan, heat the remaining oil; add the ground paste and sauté till fragrant.

❹ Stir in the chicken stock, red chillies, curry powder, snow peas, salt and pepper powder and mix well.

❺ Add the lemon juice, coconut milk and one-fourth cup of water and bring the mixture to a boil.

❻ To serve, place the boiled noodles in individual serving bowls; add the chicken, spring onions, cucumber, fresh coriander and fresh mint.

❼ Pour the hot soup over the noodles, fix half a lemon on the rim and serve immediately.

mutton dhansaak

Ingredients

450 grams boneless lean lamb or
mutton, cubed

¼ cup split pigeon peas

¼ cup split red lentils

2 medium onions, sliced

1 inch ginger, chopped

5-6 garlic cloves, chopped

10 black peppercorns

2 green chillies, slit and seeded

½ teaspoon turmeric powder

1 teaspoon red chilli powder

100 grams pumpkin, cut into ½-inch cubes

3 medium brinjals, cut into ½-inch cubes

1 large potato, cut into ½-inch cubes

1 teaspoon salt

¼ medium bunch (75 grams) fresh
fenugreek, chopped

10-15 fresh mint leaves, chopped

2 medium tomatoes, chopped

2 tablespoons *dhansaak masala*

3 tablespoons tamarind pulp

2 tablespoons chopped fresh coriander

Method

❶ Soak the pigeon peas and red lentils in two cups water for thirty minutes. Drain.

❷ Heat a non-stick pan. Add the onions and roast on low heat for two to three minutes. Add the ginger and garlic and stir for three to four minutes.

❸ Add the lamb and continue to cook for eight to ten minutes, until the meat is lightly browned on all sides.

❹ Stir in the peppercorns, chillies, turmeric powder and chilli powder and mix. Add the soaked pigeon peas and red lentils. Mix well.

❺ Add the pumpkin, brinjals, potato, salt and three-and-a-half cups of water. Bring to a boil and cook for ten minutes.

❻ Stir in the fresh fenugreek and mint, followed by the tomatoes. Cover and cook over low heat until the mutton is cooked – this may take thirty to forty-five minutes. If you are using a pressure cooker, cook till pressure is released six times (six whistles.)

❼ Once the lamb is cooked, switch off the heat and remove the meat from the mixture. Stir in the *dhansaak masala* and tamarind pulp. Let the mixture cool.

❽ Pour the mixture into a blender and process till smooth. Transfer back into the pan and add the lamb. If necessary, adjust the consistency by adding water. Sprinkle the fresh coriander and cook for a further five minutes.

❾ Serve hot with brown rice.

This is a perfect one-dish meal and is easily prepared using a pressure cooker. Serve with a salad.

dal gosht

Ingredients

¼ cup split Bengal gram, soaked

2 tablespoons split pigeon peas, soaked

2 tablespoons split red lentils, soaked

250 grams boneless mutton, cut into
1-inch cubes

1 tablespoon oil

½ teaspoon cumin seeds

2 green chillies, slit

2 teaspoons ginger paste

2 teaspoons garlic paste

1 large onion, chopped

1 medium tomato, chopped

Salt to taste

1 teaspoon red chilli powder

1 teaspoon coriander powder

1 teaspoon cumin powder

¼ teaspoon turmeric powder

¼ teaspoon *garam masala* powder

½ tablespoon lemon juice

2 tablespoons chopped fresh coriander

Method

❶ Heat the oil in a pressure cooker. Add the cumin seeds and green chillies and sauté till the cumin seeds begin to change colour. Add the ginger paste and garlic paste and sauté for half a minute.

❷ Add the onion and sauté till golden brown. Add the tomato and salt and continue to sauté for two more minutes.

❸ Add the chilli, coriander, cumin and turmeric powders and mutton and sauté for two minutes. Stir in the *garam masala* powder.

❹ Add one cup of water and bring to a boil. Seal the cooker with the lid and cook till the pressure is released twice (two whistles).

❺ When the pressure has reduced completely, remove the lid and add the soaked *dals* and four-and-a-half cups of water. Bring to a boil, replace the lid and cook till the pressure is released eight to ten times (eight to ten whistles).

❻ Once again allow the pressure to reduce completely. Remove the lid, stir and mash the *dals* lightly. Stir in the lemon juice and fresh coriander and simmer for five minutes.

❼ Serve hot.

Dal Gosht is a traditional recipe enriched with high-protein ingredients like *dal* and mutton.

dum ki machhli

Ingredients

600 grams king fish fillets,
cut into 2-inch cubes

2 teaspoons ginger-garlic paste

1 tablespoon lemon juice

Salt to taste

3 cloves

2 one-inch cinnamon sticks

½ teaspoon caraway seeds

5 green cardamoms

6 cashew nuts

2 teaspoons cudpah nuts

2 teaspoons poppy seeds

½ cup browned onions

1½ cups thick yogurt

½ cup grated *khoya/mawa*

A few sprigs fresh mint, roughly torn

2 tablespoons chopped fresh coriander

2-3 green chillies, chopped

½ teaspoon turmeric powder

A few threads of saffron,
soaked in 1 tablespoon of water

1 teaspoon *garam masala* powder

3 tablespoons oil

2 lemons, cut into wedges

Method

❶ Marinate the fish pieces with the ginger-garlic paste, lemon juice and salt. Set aside for thirty minutes.

❷ Lightly roast the cloves, cinnamon, caraway seeds and cardamoms and grind to a fine powder.

❸ Dry-roast the cashew nuts, cudpah nuts and poppy seeds and grind to a fine paste.

❹ Grind the browned onions with one and a half tablespoons of yogurt to a fine paste.

❺ Whisk the remaining yogurt with the grated *khoya* till smooth.

❻ In a bowl, mix togehter the cashew nut paste, browned onion paste, freshly ground *masala* powder and yogurt-*khoya* mixture. Add the fresh mint, fresh coriander and green chillies.

❼ Add the turmeric powder, saffron and *garam masala* powder and whisk again. Add half the oil and whisk once more.

❽ Apply the marinade to the fish pieces and set aside for fifteen minutes.

❾ Heat the remaining oil in a non-stick frying pan and stir-fry the fish along with the marinade. Turn and cook on the other side and cook for seven to eight minutes, or till both sides are equally done.

❿ Serve hot garnished with the lemon wedges.

Fish marinated in an exotic mix of yogurt, nuts, poppy seeds and *khoya*. The final dish is something memorable.

kolhapuri sukka chicken

Ingredients

1 whole (1 kilogram) chicken,
skinned and cut into 12 pieces

1 teaspoon Kolhapuri Dry Chutney (page 126)

1 tablespoon sesame seeds

2 tablespoons poppy seeds

6-8 black peppercorns

1 teaspoon caraway seeds

1 inch cinnamon

3-4 green cardamoms

1 black cardamom

4-5 cloves

1 blade mace

1 tablespoon grated dried coconut

1 tablespoon melon seeds

8-10 Bedgi red chillies

1 inch ginger

6-8 garlic cloves

2 tablespoons oil

3-4 dried red chillies

3 medium onions, chopped

¼ teaspoon turmeric powder

A pinch grated nutmeg

Salt to taste

2 tablespoons chopped fresh coriander

Method

❶ Dry-roast the sesame seeds, poppy seeds, peppercorns, caraway seeds, cinnamon, green and black cardamoms, cloves and mace separately. Cool and grind along with the dried coconut, melon seeds and red chillies, adding a little water, to a fine paste. Grind the ginger and garlic to a fine paste.

❷ Heat the oil in a deep non-stick pan and add the dried red chillies. Stir-fry briefly, drain on absorbent paper and reserve for garnish. Add the onions to the same oil and sauté till golden brown. Add the ginger-garlic paste and cook on medium heat for a few seconds.

❸ Stir in the ground paste and cook for three to four minutes on medium heat, stirring frequently. Add the chicken, mix well and cook on high heat, stirring continuously, for two to three minutes. Add half a cup of water and continue cooking on medium heat for three to four minutes, stirring frequently.

❹ Add the turmeric powder, grated nutmeg, Kolhapuri chutney and salt. Mix well and cook till chicken is completely cooked, stirring frequently.

❺ The *masala* should be quite thick and dry. Serve hot, garnished with the fresh coriander and fried red chillies.

Kolhapuri food is known for its generous use of chillies making it fiery hot. My recipe here is spicy but not so much that it overwhelms the taste buds. Coconut gives the dish a special flavour.

quick jeera chicken

Ingredients

1 teaspoon cumin seeds

1 chicken (800 grams), skinned
and cut into 1½-inch pieces

1 tablespoon oil

4-5 green chillies, sliced

2 medium onions, sliced

1 teaspoon red chilli powder

½ teaspoon turmeric powder

Salt to taste

1 tablespoon lemon juice

2 tablespoons chopped fresh coriander

1 tablespoon hand-torn fresh mint

Method

❶ Heat the oil in a non-stick *kadai*. Add the cumin seeds and sauté till they begin to change colour. Add the green chillies and onions and sauté till golden brown.

❷ Add the chicken and stir. Cover and cook on medium heat for ten minutes.

❸ Add the chilli powder, turmeric powder and salt and mix well. Cover again and cook for another ten minutes or till the chicken is completely cooked.

❹ Add the lemon juice, fresh coriander and fresh mint and mix.

❺ Serve hot with *roti*.

Short work in the kitchen but with excellent results! Have this ideally with *roti*, *pao* or brown bread.

fish in banana leaves

Ingredients

4 (100 grams each) pomfret fillets
Salt to taste
4 tablespoons lemon juice
1 cup chopped fresh coriander
4 green chillies, roughly chopped
¼ cup grated coconut
1 small onion, chopped
3 teaspoons cumin seeds
6-8 garlic cloves
3-4 banana leaves

Method

❶ Cut the fish fillets into two-inch by one and a half inch pieces.
❷ Sprinkle the salt and half the lemon juice and set aside for half an hour.
❸ Grind the coriander, green chillies, coconut, onion, cumin seeds and garlic to a fine paste. Add the salt and remaining lemon juice. Mix well.
❹ Apply the ground paste to the fish fillets and marinate for at least fifteen minutes.
❺ Cut the banana leaves into four pieces each.
❻ Place one marinated fish piece on each piece of banana leaf along with a little of the ground paste and fold it.
❼ Steam the fish in a steamer for fifteen minutes and serve hot.

doi machch

Ingredients

600 grams *rohu* fish, cut into 1-inch thick slices
1 cup yogurt
Salt to taste
1 tablespoon oil
2 bay leaves
4-6 cloves
3-4 green cardamoms
2 small onions, grated
3 green chillies, slit

Method

❶ Whisk the yogurt, add salt and marinate the fish in this mixture for twenty minutes.
❷ Heat the oil in a non-stick *kadai* and add the bay leaves, cloves and cardamoms. Cook for fifteen seconds. Add the onions and sauté on medium heat for five to seven minutes.
❸ Add the chillies and fish along with the yogurt. Bring to a boil. Cover and cook on low heat for seven to eight minutes.
❹ Serve hot.

Some people like this recipe cooked in mustard oil. If you wish to use mustard oil, heat it to smoking point, cool it and then use as normal.

dahi ka gosht

Ingredients

800 grams boneless, lean mutton, cubed

1½ cups yogurt

3 teaspoons oil

2 medium onions, sliced

2 teaspoons ginger paste

2 teaspoons garlic paste

5 green chillies, minced

Salt to taste

2 bay leaves

1 teaspoon coriander powder

1 teaspoon cumin powder

½ teaspoon mace-cardamom powder

2 tablespoons chopped fresh coriander

Method

❶ Heat one teaspoon of oil in a non-stick *kadai* and sauté the onions on medium heat till brown. Grind the onions to a fine paste.

❷ Marinate the mutton in a mixture of the yogurt, ginger paste, garlic paste, chillies and salt for one hour, preferably in a refrigerator.

❸ Heat the remaining oil in a pressure cooker and add the bay leaves.

❹ Add the marinated mutton and cook till the gravy comes to a boil. Stir in the coriander powder, cumin powder, browned onion paste and half a cup of water.

❺ Seal the cooker with the lid and cook till the pressure is released six times (six whistles). Remove the lid when the pressure has reduced completely and sprinkle the mace-cardamom powder over the mutton.

❻ Serve hot, garnished with the fresh coriander.

rice with stewed mushrooms and chicken

Ingredients

3 cups cooked rice

10 fresh button mushrooms, quartered

¾ cup cooked and shredded boneless chicken

1½ tablespoons light soy sauce

¼ teaspoon MSG (optional)

2 teaspoons wine or sherry (optional)

½ teaspoon black pepper powder

Salt to taste

1 tablespoon oil

2 spring onions, chopped

5-6 garlic cloves, chopped

1 inch ginger, chopped

1 cup Chicken Stock (page 126)

2 teaspoons cornflour

1 egg omelette, cut into strips

Method

❶ In a bowl, combine the mushrooms and chicken. Add the soy sauce, MSG, wine, pepper powder and salt and mix well.

❷ Heat the oil in a non-stick pan and sauté the spring onions, garlic and ginger till lightly browned.

❸ Add the chicken and mushroom mixture and stir-fry for one minute.

❹ Add the chicken stock and bring to a boil. Add the cornflour mixed with two tablespoons of water, and stir till the sauce thickens.

❺ Arrange the rice on a serving dish and pour the gravy over it.

❻ Garnish with the omelette strips and serve hot.

Ever been stuck with extra steamed rice in the fridge? Transform it with this delightful chicken and mushroom medley.

yogurt and chiku ice cream

Ingredients

1 cup drained (hung) yogurt

6 medium *chikus*

¼ cup powdered sugar

3 tablespoons honey

½ cup condensed milk

8-10 walnut kernels, crushed

Method

❶ Peel and pit the *chikus*. Place them in a processor/blender and crush.

❷ Add the drained yogurt and powdered sugar and mix. Add the honey and process again.

❸ Add the condensed milk and mix. Finally add the crushed walnuts and mix.

❹ Transfer the mixture into an ice cream tin and level the top.

❺ Place the tin in the deep freezer to set.

❻ When firmly set, scoop out into individual bowls and serve.

Yogurt is an excellent alternative to fresh cream.

very low-fat brownies

Ingredients

3 tablespoons cocoa powder

½ cup wholewheat flour

½ cup refined flour

½ teaspoon baking powder

½ teaspoon soda bicarbonate

1 cup caster sugar

½ cup milk

2 egg whites, beaten

1 teaspoon vanilla essence

1½ tablespoons oil

Method

❶ Preheat an oven to 180°C/350°F/Gas Mark 4. Line an eight-inch square cake tin with butter paper.

❷ Sift the cocoa powder, wholewheat flour, refined flour, baking powder and soda bicarbonate into a bowl.

❸ Stir in the caster sugar, then beat in the milk, egg whites, vanilla essence and oil until thoroughly combined.

❹ Pour the mixture into the prepared tin.

❺ Bake in the preheated oven for about twenty-five minutes or until just firm to the touch. Leave in the tin until completely cooled.

❻ Using a sharp knife, cut into sixteen squares, then remove from the tin using a spatula.

fruit kababs

Ingredients

1 large apple, cut into 1½-inch pieces

1 large kiwi fruit, cut into 1½-inch pieces

2 large bananas, cut into 1½-inch pieces

2 slices pineapple, cut into 1½-inch pieces

5 plums, cut into 1½-inch pieces

Marinade

¼ cup honey

3 tablespoons lemon juice

3 tablespoons brown sugar

Salt to taste

2 tablespoons oil

Method

❶ To prepare the marinade, place the honey in a bowl. Add the lemon juice, brown sugar, salt and oil and mix well.

❷ Thread the fruit pieces onto skewers in the following order: apple, kiwi, banana, pineapple, plum. Pour some marinade over the fruits.

❸ Heat a *tawa* on high heat; place the skewers on it and cook. Keep rotating the skewers. Pour the remaining marinade over and cook till the fruits are golden on all sides.

❹ Serve hot with Pineapple Chutney (page 126).

anjeer ka meetha

Ingredients

250 grams dried figs
250 grams seedless dried dates
¼ cup milk powder
4-5 almonds, roasted and slivered

Method

❶ Soak the figs in three cups of water for three to four hours. Boil the figs in the same water in which they were soaked for three to five minutes.
❷ Remove from heat, drain and cool slightly. Reserve some figs and pureé the rest. Chop the reserved figs.
❸ Chop the dates roughly and place them in two cups of hot water for fifteen to twenty minutes. Drain and pureé.
❹ Mix the two pureés and add milk powder. Mix well and cook on low heat for fifteen to twenty minutes or till well-blended.
❺ Add the chopped figs and simmer for two to three minutes longer.
❻ Serve, garnished with almond slivers.

kesari phirni

Ingredients

2 cups milk
3 tablespoons rice, soaked
A few saffron threads
3-4 pistachios
½ cup sugar
¼ teaspoon green cardamom powder

Method

❶ Boil the milk and set aside. Drain and grind the rice coarsely.

❷ Soak the saffron in one tablespoon of milk. Blanch the pistachios, peel and cut into slivers.

❸ Add the rice paste to the milk and cook, stirring continuously so that there are no lumps.

❹ Add the sugar and mix. Add the cardamom powder and saffron-flavoured milk and mix. When the mixture starts thickening take it off the heat.

❺ Pour into *kasoras* (earthenware bowls) that have been soaked in water for some time.

❻ Garnish with pistachio slivers and place in a refrigerator to chill.

❼ Served chilled.

saeb aur sooji halwa

Ingredients

2 large apples, thinly sliced
+ 1 large apple, puréed
½ cup semolina
1 cup milk
⅓ cup sugar
½ teaspoon green cardamom powder
A generous pinch of saffron
5-6 pistachios, blanched and slivered

Method

❶ Dry-roast the semolina lightly, taking care that it does not change colour.

❷ Boil the milk with one cup of water in a deep pan. Add the sugar, cardamom powder and half the saffron.

❸ Slowly add the semolina and cook, stirring, till it becomes semi-dry. Add the puréed apple and cook for two to three minutes.

❹ Divide into four portions. Pack each portion tightly into a bowl, turn it upside down onto a serving plate to unmould.

❺ Decorate with apple slices, pistachios and saffron.

A comforting dish on a cold winter's day. The best part is that unlike traditional halwas this is easy to make even without added fat!

saeb ki kheer

Ingredients

2 medium apples
5 cups milk
5 tablespoons sugar
½ teaspoon green cardamom powder
10-12 almonds

Method

❶ Bring the milk to a boil in a thick-bottomed pan and simmer till it thickens.
❷ Grate the apples coarsely without peeling.
❸ Heat a pan, add the grated apples and cook on medium heat. Add the sugar and stew the apples till the sugar melts. Continue to cook till most of the moisture evaporates.
❹ Add some of the reduced milk. As the mixture thickens add the remaining milk and cook till the *kheer* thickens some more.
❺ Add the cardamom powder and almonds and continue to cook till the kheer thickens to the desired consistency.
❻ Cool and chill before serving.

chicken stock

Boil 200 grams chicken bones in water for 5 minutes. Drain and discard water. Boil blanched bones with a roughly chopped carrot, celery stalk, leek, 2-3 parsley stalks, 6-7 black peppercorns, 5-6 cloves, 1 bay leaf and 10 cups of water. Remove any scum which rises to the surface and replace it with more cold water. Simmer for at least 1 hour. Remove from heat, strain, cool and store in a refrigerator till further use.

vegetable stock

Peel, wash and chop 1 onion, ½ medium carrot, 2-3inch stalk celery and 2-3 garlic cloves. Place in a pan with 1 bay leaf, 5-6 peppercorns, 2-3 cloves and five cups of water and bring to a boil. Lower heat and simmer for 15 minutes and strain. Cool and store in a refrigerator till further use.

coconut milk

Process 1 cup grated fresh coconut in a blender with ¼ cup warm water. Pass the ground coconut through a piece of muslin or strainer pressing firmly to extract all the juice, or first milk. Add ¼ cup of warm water to the strained coconut to get the second, thinner milk from the same solids.

green chutney

Grind together 1 cup fresh coriander leaves, ½ cup fresh mint leaves, 2-3 green chillies, black salt to taste, ¼ teaspoon sugar and 1 tablespoon lemon juice to a smooth paste using a little water if required.

date and tamarind chutney

Wash, stone and chop 15-20 dates. Dry-roast 2 teaspoons cumin seeds and ¼ teaspoon fennel seeds. Cool and grind to a powder. Cook dates, 1 cup tamarind pulp, cumin and fennel powder, ½ cup jaggery, 2 teaspoons red chilli powder, 1 teaspoon dried ginger powder (soonth), black salt, salt and 4 cups of water till thick.

kolhapuri dry chutney

Dry-roast 1 cup coriander seeds, 1 tablespoon cumin seeds,1 tablespoon sesame seeds, 8-10 black peppercorns, ½ inch stick cinnamon, 10 cloves and 1 teaspoon fennel seeds. Set aside to cool. Roast ½ cup grated dried coconut till it turns reddish. Set aside to cool. Heat 2 tablespoons olive oil and fry roughly chopped 2 medium onions, 10 garlic cloves and 1 cup chopped fresh coriander leaves on low heat till well browned and crisp. Set aside to cool. Mix all the ingredients together and grind to a fine powder. Mix with 1 cup red chilli powder. Store when completely cooled in an airtight container preferably in a refrigerator.

pineapple chutney

Peel and cut 1 medium pineapple into small pieces and place in a thick-bot tomed pan. Add 1 teaspoon ginger paste, mix well and cook for 5 minutes. Add 1 tablespoon sugar and 2 tablespoons raisins and cook. Add ½ teaspoon roasted *panch phoron* powder, ½ teaspoon crushed red chillies and salt to taste. Add ½ cup water and cook for 5 minutes on low heat. Sprinkle ½ teaspoon roasted *panch phoron* powder and serve.

Note: *Panch phoron* is a mixture of ¼ teaspoon mustard seeds, ¼ teaspoon cumin seeds, ¼ teaspoon fenugreek seeds, ¼ teaspoon fennel seeds and ¼ teaspoon onion seeds.

chilli oil

Cook 6 tablespoons of chopped dried red chillies in 1¼ cups of groundnut oil, on low heat, for at least 10 minutes. When completely cold, stir in 2-3 tablespoons of red chilli powder and 1-2 tablespoons of sesame oil. Cover and leave to stand for at least 12 hours. Strain into a sterilized bottle and store in a cool, dark place.

Glossary

ENGLISH	HINDI	ENGLISH	HINDI
Almonds	Badam	Chillies, green	Hari mirch
Apple	Saeb	Chillies, red button	Sookha gol mirch
Asafoetida	Hing	Cinnamon	Dalchini
Baby corn	Chhote bhutte	Cloves	Laung
Banana	Kela	Coconut, dried	Khopra
Basil, fresh	Tulsi ki pattiyan	Coconut, fresh	Nariyal
Bay leaves	Tez patta	Coconut, fresh tender	Malai
Bean sprouts	Ankurit moong	Coriander seeds	Dhania
Beans, black-eyed	Chauli	Coriander, fresh	Hara dhania
Bitter gourds	Karele	Cottage cheese	Paneer
Brinjal, baby	Chhote baingan	Cream	Malai
Brinjals	Baingan	Cucumbers	Kakdi
Broad beans	Sem/bakla	Cudpah seeds	Chironji
Butter	Makkhan	Cumin seeds	Jeera
Cabbage	Patta gobhi	Curry leaves	Kadhi patta
Capsicum, green	Hari Shimla mirch	Dates	Khajur
Capsicum, red	Lal Shimla mirch	Egg	Anda
Capsicum, yellow	Pili Shimla mirch	Fennel seeds	Saunf
Caraway	Shahi jeera	Fenugreek leaves, dried	Kasuri methi
Cardamoms, black	Badi elaichi	Fenugreek seeds	Methi dana
Cardamoms, green	Chhoti elaichi	Fenugreek, fresh	Methi
Carom seeds	Ajwain	Figs	Anjeer
Carrot	Gajar	French beans	Farasi
Cashew nuts	Kaju	Gamboge rind	Kokum
Caster sugar	Pisi hui shakkar	Garlic	Lehsun
Cauliflower	Phool gobhi	Ginger, dried	Sonth
Celery	Ajmud	Ginger, fresh	Adrak
Chickpeas	Kabuli chana	Gram flour	Besan
Chillies, dried red	Sookhi lal mirch	Gram, Bengal fresh green	Taaze hare chane
Chillies, fresh red	Taazi lal mirch	Gram, Bengal split	Chana dal

ENGLISH	HINDI	ENGLISH	HINDI
Gram, Bengal whole black	Kale chane	Poppy seeds	Khuskhus
Gram, black split skinless	Dhuli urad dal	Potatoes	Aloo
Gram, green split	Moong	Prawns	Jheenga
Guava	Amrud	Pumpkin, red	Lal kumbda
Honey	Shahad	Radish	Mooli
Jaggery	Gur	Raisins	Kishmish
Ladies' fingers	Bhindi	Refined flour	Maida
Lemon	Nimbu	Rice, parboiled	Ukda chawal
Lentils, red split	Masoor dal	Rice, puffed	Kurmura
Lettuce	Salad ke patte	Saffron	Kesar
Mace	Javitri	Sago	Sabudana
Mango, ripe	Aam	Salt, black	Kala namak
Mango, unripe	Keri	Salt, rock	Sendha namak
Mango, unripe, dried and powdered	Amchur	Sapota	Chiku
Melon	Tarbooj	Semolina	Sooji/rawa
Mint leaves, fresh	Pudina ke taazi pattiyan	Sesame seeds	Til
Mushroom	Khumb	Shallots	Chhote pyaaz
Mustard seeds	Rai	Spinach	Palak
Mutton	Gosht	Spring onion	Hara pyaaz
Nutmeg	Jaiphal	Spring onion greens	Hare pyaaz ki pattiyan
Olives	Jaitun	Sweetcorn kernels	Makai ke dane
Onion seeds	Kalonji	Tamarind	Imli
Parsley	Ajmoda	Tomato purée	Pise hue tamatar
Peanuts	Moongphali	Tomatoes	Tamatar
Peas, green	Taaze hare matar	Tomatoes, cherry	Chote tamatar
Peppercorns, black	Kali mirch	Turmeric powder	Haldi
Peppercorns, white	Safed mirch	Vetiver	Khus
Pigeon peas, fresh green	Hara toovar	Vinegar	Sirka
Pigeon peas, split	Toovar dal/arhar dal	Walnut	Akhrot
Pine nuts	Chilgoza	Wholewheat flour	Atta
Pineapple	Ananas	Yogurt	Dahi
Pistachios	Pista		
Pomegranate kernels	Anar ke dane		